John Campbell Miller

Builder of Fancy Homes in Rural West Virginia

Becky Hatcher Crabtree
and
Fred Ziegler

35th Star Publishing
Charleston, West Virginia
www.35thstar.com

Copyright. © 2021 by Becky Hatcher Crabtree, Fred Ziegler.
All Rights Reserved.
First edition, 2021.
Printed in the United States of America.

No part of this publication may be reproduced, distributed or transmitted in any form or by any means, including photocopying, recording, or other electronic or mechanical methods, without the prior written permission of the publisher, except in the case of brief quotations embodied in critical reviews and certain other noncommercial uses permitted by copyright law.

ISBN-13: 978-1-7378575-1-8
ISBN-10: 1-7378575-1-0
Library of Congress Control Number: 2021946366

35th Star Publishing
Charleston, West Virginia
www.35thstar.com

On the front cover: Image of John Campbell Miller, courtesy of Johnny Greene.
Marshall B. Dunn family and home, courtesy of Marshall Lee Dunn.
On the back cover: E.I. Terry home, courtesy of Pamela Agee Jackson.
Cover design by Studio 6 Sense
Interior design by 35th Star Publishing

"People are never really gone
as long as there is someone who remembers,
and in that way, my ancestors live on."

Georgie (Knowles) McDaniel (1904-2000)
wife of A. Cecil McDaniel

Table of Contents

Acknowledgments ix
Photo Credits xi
Introduction 1
Area Map 3

1 - Beginnings of a Housing Boom 5
Table 1: Definition of Architectural Terms
Table 2: Hallmarks of Style
2 - Greenville and West Along the Indian Creek Valley 21
3 - The Lower Hans Creek Valley 45
4 - Orchard and Pine Grove Road 77
5 - The Seneca Trail from Lindside to Fountain Springs 91
6 - Peterstown 111
7 - Cashmere and Ballard 129
8 - Red Sulphur Springs and Indian Mills 149
9 - McDowell County Homes 167
10 - Concluding Observations 171

Appendices Introduction 175
Appendix A: Original List of Miller Houses 177
Appendix B: Updated List of Miller Houses 179
References 181
Notes 187
Index 191
Image Index 199
About the Authors 203

Acknowledgments

Thank you to the following for their time and knowledge. They guided us to fascinating times and people of the past.

Rusty Agee
Robert Allen
Bill Bailey
Judith Bair
Jason Ballard
Jeff Ballard
Lou Ballard
Nancy Belcher
Leigh W. Boggess
Donny L. Bradley
Jeremy Brown
Petrie Brown
Sonny and Betty Brown
Connie Broyles
Nora Lee Broyles
Jason Buckland
Mary Burks
Gladys Larew Carter
Lucy Comer
Raymond Comer
Alicia and Bobby Coulter
Joey Dunn
Marshall Dunn
Bert and Paula Ellison
Elizabeth Francis
Karen Gore
Johnny Greene
Valerie Hansbarger
Suzie and Howdy Henritz
Jarrod Hines
Jodi Hines-Bowers
Mike Hines

Billy Hodges
Otuse Huffman
Clark and Linda Humphreys
Joy Huntley
Pam Jackson
Ellen Spangler Johnson
Maury Johnson
Wayne Johnson
Grover Jones
Susan Ballard King
Charles Larew
Robert Larew
Wib and Irene Larew
Michael Lentz
Cathy McDaniel Levandowski
Mike Lively
Matthew Long
Reba Long
Tammy Long
Angie Terry Mann
Paula Oliver Mann
Sean Mann
Monnie Marten
Trixie Marten
Jim McGrady
Nallie McKenzie
Craig Mohler
Clayton Moore
Cynthia Morris
Ruth Miller Mann Pence
Otis Pence
Charlie Pitzer

Vernessa Pontius
Jodie Posey
Stan Presley
Faye Ramsey
Christy Reece
Ron Ripley
Catharine Rolling
Rusty Sammons
Alison Simpson
Erica Smith
Alan Spangler
Johnny Spangler
Aaron and Alana Terry
Johnny and Linda Terry
Layman and Laurie Thomas
Carol and Norman Thompson
Norman Thomas
Lucy Toney
Anita Tracy
Shirley Green Ulaki
Jack Vickers
John Wickline
Robbie Wickline
David Wright

Photo Credits

Beckley Sunday Register   113
Blair, Judith   51
Bluefield Daily Telegraph   124
Boggess, Leigh   113
Brown, Petrie   52-53
Broyles, Nora Lee   143-44
Burks, Mary   80
Carter, Gladys   56
Dumont, John W.   153
Dunn, Joey   130
Dunn, Marshall Lee   135
Dunn, Mary South   137
Find-a-Grave   37
First National Bank of Peterstown, Anniversary Calendar   118, 120-21, 127
Greene, Irene   6, 15, 23, 26 32, 39, 40, 58, 63, 67, 72-73, 81, 83, 93, 108, 131, 136, 139, 156-57, 160
Greene, Johnny   73
Hines, Jarrod   138-39
Humphreys, Clark   10, 12, 54-56, 70-71, 73-76, 78, 82-83, 142, 154-55
Jackson, Pam Agee   114, 146
Johnson, Ellen Spangler   127
Larew, Robert   57, 59, 60
Levandowski, Cathy McDaniel   95-99
McDaniel, Bonnie Bradley   99
McGrady, James   47, 49
McKenzie, Nally   119
Martin, Monnie   79
Monroe County Bicentennial Committee   112, 115
Monroe County Historical Society   19, 23, 30, 31, 103, 117, 162, 165
Oliver Photography   143
Owens, S. T.   109
Phipps, Jennie   38
Simpson, Alison   123-25
Skidmore, Jill   144
West, Kevin Thomas   25
WVU Libraries   24, 27-28, 31, 51, 65-69
Ziegler, Fred   105-6
[All other photographs not listed here are by Becky Crabtree]

Introduction

Surrounded by beautiful farmland and framed by hills and mountains rising 2,000 feet above the valley floor, John Campbell Miller constructed elaborate Victorian homes in the western part of Monroe County, West Virginia.

Throughout his 37 years as a homebuilder, beginning in 1886, he constructed upward of 100 houses ranging from the elegant Queen Anne style to cozy Craftsman cottages, most within an eight-mile radius of his home in Wesley Hollow. He also erected public buildings, including schools, churches, and stores as well as hundreds of small bungalows in the company towns of nearby counties.

Many of the homes remain standing and most are still lovingly tended by their occupants and admired by neighbors and passersby. It is not surprising that Miller's descendants have maintained a list of these structures as well as a photographic file. These treasures form the basis for this book and the opportunity to peek into the world of the builders of our great-grandfathers' time, which surprisingly turns out to have been highly organized, thanks to the developing catalog houses.

Miller was the eldest of 11 children, and he and Lillie Belle Miller, his first wife, raised another seven, all in Wesley Hollow, a small branch of Hans Creek, in western Monroe County. His commuting distance, by horse and wagon, was evidently eight miles, to judge by where we find examples of his work. After her death in 1922, he moved west to Huntington, remarried, and lived out his 95 years as a house painter and small-job carpenter. He commuted in a 1925 Model T Ford.

Monroe County lies astride two valleys, the James River and the New River, which cross the Allegheny Mountains from the east. These were the pathways of the pioneers of the 1750s. When they arrived, they must have been surprised to find farmland already conditioned by Native American farming activity.[1] Agriculture has been the mainstay of Monroe ever since although it was not until the 1870s that the railroad arrived, and provided the first easy route to the markets of the East Coast. As the farm population increased, new homes were needed, and it was then that Miller began his work.

More recently, the population of Monroe County has remained relatively constant, a fact bemoaned by politicians, but welcomed by preservationists and domestic architecture buffs. It seems the avenues of transportation and progress have skirted this area, starting with the railroads and continuing with the Interstate highway system. However, it does mean that the houses, farms, mills as well as some 19th century resort spas and the lovely bucolic scenery have remained, much to the delight of the traveler and photographer, as well as to those who make Monroe County their home.

Remarkably, house styles of this period are diverse and have decorative elements that would have been difficult and time consuming for the local builder to generate. Moreover, we find in traveling throughout this country that the styles of the period are replicated again and again, and the catalog companies dictated the styles by supplying both the plans and also the decorative elements to apply to those plans. The interest in this subject matter goes way beyond any county boundary. You may very well have grown up in a kit house, but if not you most certainly pass them on your way to work or shop. They are found in concentric zones around many villages, each zone recording the successive historical interval which it represents.

The location of the Miller houses is also discussed in the following chapter. The information provided includes the roads along which the buildings are situated and they are also listed in the Appendix. We stop short of providing the detailed locations to protect the privacy of the homeowners. However, it should be possible to identify the buildings by driving along the roads with the pictures in hand, just as we did initially. You will have no problem identifying these homes because most of them stand out from the landscape.

The body of the text consists of pictures of each building together with a description of the house and its history insofar as we have been able to learn it from the residents. Each group of about nine buildings constitutes a chapter which starts with a short summary of the history of the area, with special reference to the conditions that existed about the time Miller worked there.

If you visit the area, some concept of the underlying geology will help in understanding the scenery. Monroe County spans one of the most important tectonic boundaries in eastern North America, the margin of the collision zone with the southern hemisphere continent of Gondwana, about 260 million years ago.

The deformed rocks of this zone extend throughout the Appalachian Mountains to just west of U.S. Route 219, so Peters Mountain, the 3,500-foot-high mountain range along the east side of the county, alternates with long linear valleys reflecting the axes of the folds and faults that characterize the deformation. The sandstone formations are exceptionally hard and form the mountains whereas the shale and limestone are more easily eroded and form the valleys.

To the west the topography is more subdued and random but dissected by streams such as Indian Creek, Hans Creek and Brush Creek. The flood plains of these creeks are well farmed, but so are the flat-topped plateau elements which are underlain and supported by sandstone layers. In general, level ground is in short supply in West Virginia, but Monroe County is well provided with this farmer-friendly topography.

INTRODUCTION 3

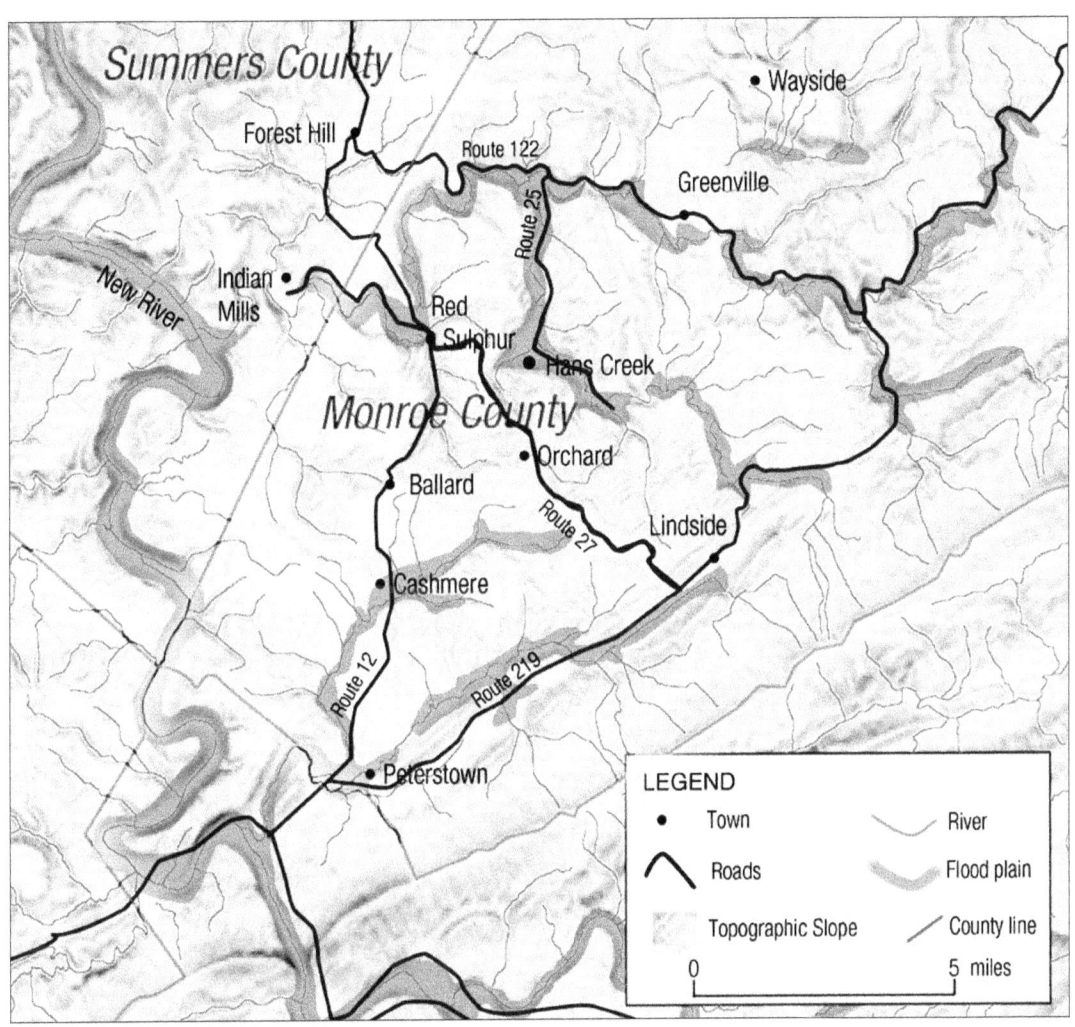

*Western Monroe County, West Virginia,
showing towns and roads discussed in the text.*

1

Beginnings of a Housing Boom

John Campbell Miller (1864-1960) was the first-born of Wilson Mann Miller and Rebecca Jane Campbell, Monroe County parents who lived in Greenbrier County during the Civil War. At the time, Wilson drove an ammunition wagon for the Confederate States of America's Chapman's Battery. After the war, the family moved back to Monroe and settled near Red Sulphur Springs in a branch of beautiful Hans Creek Valley called Wesley Hollow. The family was expanded by 14 more children over the next 20 years.

Miller's building career began in 1886 and he married Lillie Belle, maiden name Miller, in 1890. They raised a family of seven, but Lillie died in 1922 and by 1923 John had moved to Huntington, West Virginia, and later married Lennie Keatley, a childhood sweetheart.

His house-building activities in Monroe, the subject of this book, spanned 37 years and during this time, he built 100 houses by his own estimate, together with several churches, stores, and schoolhouses.

"Carpenter John," as he was known, lived to be 95 years old and during his later years, lived in Huntington. He attracted the attention of reporters because he continued to work and, in fact, drove to work in a Model T Ford runabout, vintage 1925. Apparently, he did not build more houses, but as a Huntington reporter wrote, Miller kept active by "wielding a paint brush, a hammer or saw at some house. ... Mr. Miller is short of stature, but his arms and shoulders are those of a weightlifter. His hair is thick on his head, and his smile is as sunny as his laugh is hearty."[2]

Housebuilding, 1880-1920

Miller built an impressive number of fancy Victorian buildings and transitioned into the 20th century with the Craftsman and Colonial Revival styles. Many questions arise: how did he do it, did he have a crew to do the ornate turnings and scroll-saw work, and above all, who prepared the plans for these well-designed buildings, many of which feature built-in cabinetry? We know from markings on one house that the millwork came from Sears, Roebuck and Co., however, this house dates from 1907 and the famous Sears kit houses came on the market a year later. Miller's house-building career in Monroe County was half completed by that time.

"Houses from Books" by Daniel D. Reiff, written in 2000, explains the availability of architectural aids for housebuilders from 1738 to 1950. He points out that factory-made building components became available after the Civil War and that by the final

John Campbell and Lillie Belle Miller Family, circa 1905.
Front row: standing, George Dewey, b. 1898; John Campbell Miller;
Lillie Belle Miller; on mother's lap, Dorsey Gordon, b. 1904; John Clyde, b. 1900.
Back row, standing, left to right: Ray Seleska, b. 1891; Florence Mary, b. 1895.
Photo provided by Irene Greene.

two decades of the 19th century more than 100 catalogs of manufactured components were current with most of these being for residences. They offered doors, window sashes, staircase parts, builder's trimmings, columns, and many other items. Also, the railway network was being expanded and Rural Free Delivery was introduced in 1893, so early in his career Miller could have ordered the millwork from his home and had it delivered.

Building plans were easily obtained by the time Miller began work. He could have subscribed to The American Architect and Building News or bought the plan books of William T. Comstock, Architectural Publisher, New York, or George F. Barber & Co. Architects, Knoxville, Tennessee. Reprints of these latter two are available from Dover Publications and include floor plans as well as perspective drawings. These pattern books are just a few of the 151 titles in the Dover "Architecture and Design" series currently available, many of which concern domestic structures of the period of interest. In fact, they are a valuable resource for the owners of these vintage buildings contemplating restoration work. For the researcher, they provide ground truth in documenting the date of origin of the building styles as they evolved through time, as well as the terms which were used to describe them.

The full development of the kit house occurred during the career of Miller. Sears was advertising building materials in its general catalog as early as 1893. However, it was the Aladdin Company of Bay City, Michigan, that published the first catalog of precut and fitted lumber for homes in 1906. Sears followed in 1908 although the rough lumber for framing and sheathing was left for the local market. That is, the planed siding and casing for doors and windows was included in the kit, as well as the fancier millwork. At this time, Sears was providing, in addition to the general catalog, the Home Builders Catalog which had some building plans, but concentrated on the diverse parts, ranging from stained-glass windows to concrete building-block molds. The house plans and drawings were available in the Modern Homes catalog, complete with prices and estimates of the cost of building the house on the site. One could select the general plan, but choose from a number of door and cabinet styles to go with the plan. These specialized catalogs ran more than 100 pages each, so there was plenty to suit any taste.

Miller later used local companies for millwork. A multi-page order from the Minter Homes Corporation was found in the files of the Monroe County Historical Society and was sent to L. M. Campbell, owner of house No. 51, on Dec. 27, 1922. According to the West Virginia Encyclopedia, Minter was a manufacturer of ready-to-build housing, established in Huntington, in 1913. It supplied a catalog of house plans and provided house packages for entire villages throughout the South and East. It seems likely that Miller used this company for the above-mentioned houses he built in McDowell County before World War I.

It is clear Miller could purchase at least some house plans economically from a variety of sources and had no need to employ an architect. Likewise, countless patterns of fancy millwork produced by Sears and other catalog houses replaced the need for a shop full of craftsmen working lathes and scroll-saws.

But what sort of a workforce did he use to build the houses? He is responsible for up to three buildings a year, many of them impressively large and complicated. Newspaper articles mention the name of Davis A. Halstead as a partner around the turn of the century, and Otuse (Otis) Heslep in 1923. Quite likely he easily found additional workforce in the area, including the prospective owners, as we know that Jack Johnson worked with Miller to build his own house, No. 8, according to Jack's daughter.

Victorian House Styles

The definitive guide to identifying and understanding America's domestic architecture is "A Field Guide to American Houses" by Virginia Savage McAlester, written in 2018. This work has been expanded from a 1984 edition to 848 pages and covers 49 styles with many more substyles, and these range from Native American to Millenium Mansion. Each type is described from the architectural and historical perspective and is supplied with informative line drawings and an abundance of photographs of examples from various parts of the country.

The first question to be addressed is, what is a house style, and how is it possible to travel across a large country such as the United States. and recognize the same styles again and again? Were builders like Miller simply turning out products, assembly-line fashion, or was there latitude for creativity? The fact that people are still talking about his houses and marvel at their beauty shows that Miller was able to work within the system to create a stunning product. Part of the reason is that there was much to choose from as the pattern books drew on dozens of designers to create hundreds of plans, and catalog houses also had many house parts to select from. There was also latitude in the setting of the building, the paint scheme, and the modifications to the design that could be made.

Miller is best known for his Queen Anne style work. It was introduced from Britain in 1876 at the Centennial Exposition in Philadelphia and a good description of the style was given in 1881 by respected architects Ehrick Rossiter and Frank A. Wright: "The general form and arrangement of these buildings was after the Gothic manner; i.e. they were designed from the inside; the plan was the first consideration, and was made to meet the practical requirements of the times, while the exterior was left in great measure to take care of and adapt itself to the plan. Picturesqueness was aimed at … and symmetry began to be considered as no longer the essential characteristic of good architecture."[3]

Therefore, a fundamental paradigm shift in domestic architecture began as far as form was concerned. Within this constraint, McAlester recognizes four shape subtypes. For the two dozen examples among Miller's buildings, most would be classified as the "hipped roof with lower cross gables subtype." A hipped roof is one that slopes in all four directions and, in this subtype, the slope is quite steep, giving an almost pyramidal form because the ridgeline is relatively short. Another shape consideration is that Miller used "cutaway bay windows" and here two bay windows would be typically stacked above one another with the overlying gable corners projecting and supported by brackets, giving a tower-like effect. Finally, Miller frequently used wrap-around porches typically along two or three sides of the building. The end result is a roofline defined by eight to 10 planes, not including the porch which would add two or three more.

But what about decorative detailing, such as gingerbread ornamentation common with the Queen Anne style? Here, McAlester recognizes four subtypes, two of which Miller used, the Spindlework and the Free Classic subtypes. The former was popular during the Victorian era and takes advantage of the development of machine-guided lathes and scroll-saws to create elaborate ornamentation for porches, windows and gables. On porches we find fancy columns with balusters below and brackets above while fancy window patterns and complex gable ornaments were also included.

The Free Classic subtype of the Queen Anne is more subdued and represents the changing tastes into the 20th century. Here the simpler classic columns and balusters are found on the porches and Palladian windows add a decorative touch to the gables. This term refers to a grouping of three windows with the center one a little taller and rounded on the top. These motifs were seemingly borrowed from the developing Colonial Revival style, but the fancy hipped roof and cross gables remained the same as in the 19th century buildings.

Miller used other styles that we now classify as Victorian. The fact that they are less common in the data list that has been passed down may result from sampling bias, because they tended to be smaller and so do not stand out from the landscape. The term Shingle style we apply to a single house, No. 23, which has a gambrel roof with gambrel cross gables, meaning the roof surface steepens in slope from top to bottom. Like the Queen Anne style, the gables have ornaments and the porch wraps around the front and left side and has turned columns and balusters. A hallmark of the Shingle style is that shingles cover the entire building, but here they are found only on the gables, as verified by early pictures. Nonetheless, the overall shape of the structure is characteristic of the Shingle style.

We assign most of the remaining Victorian buildings to the Folk Victorian style which is a term applied to smaller buildings with gingerbread features. Here Miller applied Victorian elements to buildings that did not display the characteristic overall form of other contemporaneous styles. Finally, a word on the Richardsonian Romanesque style found in just one building, a large schoolhouse in Peterstown. This term is applied mainly to public buildings made of masonry and borrows features from the Romanesque fashion such as arches and towers used by Gothic cathedral builders.

Modern House Styles

The Colonial Revival style spans the turn of the century, and McAlester points out that "the Philadelphia Centennial of 1876 is credited with awakening an interest in our colonial architectural heritage." These homes are patterned after English and Dutch houses of the Atlantic Seaboard and remained popular into the 1950s. In the hands of Miller, we have a couple of surviving examples and they are side-gabled with symmetrical facades. The front door is supplied with multi-paned sidelights and overhead lights, and there are massive cornices defining the roof lines.

The Prairie style is one of the few styles indigenous to this country and derives from the Chicago School as led by Frank Lloyd Wright. Since many of the catalog houses

*John Campbell Miller, date unknown.
Photo provided by Clark Humphreys.*

*John Campbell Miller, in Huntington, WV, date unknown.
Photo from "Men of Monroe" file, Caperton Museum,
Monroe County, West Virginia Historical Society.*

were located there, including suppliers of kit houses, this style became popular for a brief time and the term "Four-Square" is often applied to them. These houses are two-storied, usually with a hipped roof of low pitch, and this often with a hipped dormer. The eaves are overhanging and boxed in and often there are found one or two bay window complexes while the porches have massive square columns. Oddly, one of the Monroe County houses has a tower, the hallmark of the Queen Anne style, but none of the Queen Annes do.

Finally, the Craftsman style is represented by three structures among Miller's buildings. The inspiration for this style came from the English Arts and Crafts Movement and was influenced by the rise of the middle class, the proliferation of the democratic ideal, the increase of home ownership, and an interest in natural living, according to "Craftsman Bungalows" a reprint of homes from an influential magazine (edited by Gustav Stickley from 1901-1916). This magazine was unique in its approach as it sought out designs that exemplified its ideals, but the catalog houses were quick to pick up on this style and even today this fashion is popular in design and renovation magazines. The Monroe County examples have low-pitched, side-gabled roofs with wide unenclosed eave overhangs, and exposed rafter tails with decorative braces under the gables. Windows are abundant and are typically arranged in groups of two or three. Porches are wide and supported by tapered square columns.

Economic Influences in Western Monroe

Local developments affecting the agrarian economy during the 19th century led to the increasing number of large, elaborate farmhouses built by Miller. Monroe County has a greater proportion of arable land than any other county in the state and the economy has always been based on farm products. This is especially so since there is no coal and the county has a larger proportion of relatively level ground than surrounding counties. According to Noe, "Southwest Virginians not only drove herds across the state beginning as early as 1750, but also to points as distant as Baltimore, Philadelphia, and New Orleans." He writes that small farms supplied stock or feed along the way and the larger land holders sponsored the drives.[4]

By the early 19th century, the resort springs became an important economic factor and Monroe County had more than most. Salt Sulphur Springs had a capacity of 350 beds and Sweet Springs 300, while in the area containing the Miller houses, Red Sulphur Springs could accommodate 350, and Gray Sulphur Springs near Peterstown, 200 people. They were open from June through October and drew their clientele mainly from the plantations of the Old South. Of course, this brought money, jobs, and contacts into the area and provided a demand for locally produced food. It also created a need for good roads and Virginia passed the Turnpike Act in 1817, which generally required that roads be 16 feet wide with a grade of 4 percent or less and a roadbed paved with gravel. In many cases, existing roadways were followed but straightened and upgraded and the improvements were a major benefit to the area. The state provided funding as did the resort owners while turnpike fees were used for maintenance of the system. Stagecoaches operated along these turnpikes to both convey tourists to the area

*John Campbell Miller with his 1925 Model T, date unknown.
Photo provided by Clark Humphreys.*

*John Campbell Miller and sons at the old Miller/Wesley homeplace.
Gordon Miller, John Clyde Miller. Dewey Miller, Ray Miller, John Campbell Miller,
date unknown. Photo provided by Clark Humphreys.*

as well as to shuttle them from resort to resort. All of this happened during the warmer months of the year, but also coincided with the growing season.

The heyday of the resorts was in the antebellum period and their clientele shifted to the North after the Civil War. In the meantime, the railway system was being developed. The Virginia and Tennessee Railroad was extended to Radford, Virginia by 1854 and what was to become the Chesapeake and Ohio got to Jackson River, Virginia, by 1857. The new state of West Virginia was reached after the war, as the Norfolk and Western Railroad was completed to Glen Lyn, opposite Peterstown, by 1883 and the C&O came through Lowell in 1873. As a result, western Monroe farmers within 12 miles of a railhead could drive their herds to a railyard in a day. Curiously, the operators of the Red Sulphur Springs resort preferred the Lowell connection, and even though Glen Lyn was closer, it did require a ferry to cross the New River. So, the Red Sulphur Turnpike was completed 10 miles due north to Lowell, and this served for the convenience of the passengers coming from the North.

The response of the farming community to the approach of the railways was to be expected. In 1880 there were 1,248 farms in Monroe with an average of 94 acres, and 20 years later the number had expanded to half again as many, and the acreage was expanded to 98, according to census data. No wonder there was a demand for new housing, and with families ranging from eight to 12 members large houses were the order of the day. The resorts continued to decline into the 20th century and the farming profession took up the slack. Miller had plenty of work as a result.

Geographic Context of the John Campbell Miller Buildings

The descendants of "Carpenter John," as Miller was known, have kept his memory alive over the years by making lists and photographic albums of his structures. In the files of the Monroe County Historical Society is a list of 60 homes that the museum was given several years ago. This was prepared by Florence Miller Wesley, daughter of Miller, and she "… copied them down as mother told me, adding the extra 'little bits' just as she related them to me." In 2017, Johnny Greene, grandson of Florence Wesley and son of Irene Wesley Greene gave the authors a file containing photos of 43 of these buildings. The photos are dated 1980 and 1988 as well as a few vintage photos of buildings that have disappeared over the years. The pictures had comments written on the backs which identified the buildings together with the 'little bits' from the list of 60, plus other comments. In 2019, Clark Humphreys, great-grandson of Miller, shared his picture albums containing some of the same photos but which added some new wrinkles to the original comments. Clark and his wife, Linda, were most helpful in filling out some of the history of this remarkable family.

With all this information now available, most of these buildings have been identified. The current owners have been most happy to provide more details on these beautiful structures. The information gained, including new photos as well as vintage ones, is given in the body of this book and organized into seven chapters by geographical area. The order of presentation parallels the original list for the most part, and each chapter starts with general comments on the historical background of the area and the situation there as understood during the time that John Campbell Miller was actively building, that is, from 1886 to 1923. Further data are presented in appendices, such as addresses and building dates, and also in notes, such as references to the literature.

Many of the buildings lie along a triangular array of roads, State routes 122 and 12, and U.S. Route 219 (see Figure 1). The first two, along the north and west, are part of the original turnpike system, and have been designated a Farm Heritage Trail. Route 122 follows Indian Creek and Miller houses are grouped in Greenville and to the west along an extension of the old Sweet Springs and Salt Sulphur Turnpike, and the Red Sulphur and Blue Sulphur Turnpike. Down the west side of the triangle, Route 12 retraces the old Giles, Fayette and Kanawha Turnpike, and Miller houses are found mainly in the villages of Red Sulphur, Ballard, Cashmere, and Peterstown. Moving up the northeast corridor, the road is referred to as the Seneca Trail and was so named about 1925 for an integrated automobile highway from West Virginia through Pennsylvania to New York. The name is borrowed from the Indian road which followed the Bluestone, Greenbrier, and Tygart rivers somewhat to the west. The houses lie from the communities of Fountain Springs to Lindside. In addition, Miller houses are found along county routes 25 and 27, which follow Hans Creek Valley and Pine Grove Road, respectively. In Miller's time the roads in this county were mainly unpaved and ungraded and "perhaps one-half of these could be traversed by automobile in summer."[5]

*John Campbell Miller at home in Huntington, WV, circa. 1955.
Photo provided by Irene Greene.*

Table 1
Definition of Architectural Terms
With Special Reference to the Styles Used by Miller

baluster: Short column, typically turned, supporting a porch or stair railing. The assembly may be termed a balustrade or railing.

bay window: The bump-out of a wall, trapezoidal in plan, to accommodate three windows, and it may be defined by its own roof and base. This feature is seen in the Victorian and Prairie styles.

belfry: A bell tower found on churches and schools.

brackets: Commonly used to support overhangs or to brace porch posts.

cornice: The cornice is the molding, usually decorative, along the top of a wall.

cornice-line brackets: Common decorative effect on Folk Victorian buildings.

cupola: A small tower at the center of the roof designed for decoration, ventilation, or illumination, or all of the above.

cutaway bay: A bay extending the full height of a one- or two-story wall and terminated on top by the base of a projecting gable. Miller used this feature universally in his Queen Anne houses.

dormer: A window and housing that projects from a sloping roof.

Four-Square: A two-storied house, square in plan, and typical of Prairie style houses.

eave: The lower end of the roof that overhangs the walls.

façade: The front wall of a building.

frieze: A decorative band connecting the tops of porch columns and typically constructed of repetitive turnings. This feature seems to be restricted to the Folk Victorian and Shingle style houses of Miller.

gable: The upper wall that encloses the end of a pitched roof. The roof may be side-gabled, in which case the ridgeline is parallel to the façade, front-gabled, or both.

gable-on-hip: A small vertical wall just beneath the ridgeline of a hipped roof.

gambrel roof: A two-sloped roof with a shallow upper slope, generally less than 45 degrees, above a steeper one, greater than 45 degrees. Miller used this roofline on the Shingle style house.

gingerbread ornamentation: Fancy decorative effects used on houses during the late 19th century.

hipped roof: A roof with the ends inclined as well as the sides. In other words, it slopes in all four directions and may or may not have a ridge line. A steep hipped roof with short ridge line is typical of the Queen Anne style, and a shallow hipped roof of pyramidal shape is characteristic of the Prairie style.

hipped dormer: A dormer with roofs sloping in all three directions used in Prairie style buildings.

hip-on-gable: An incomplete hipped roof such that the end gables have a trapezoidal form. This feature is used to "soften" the profile of a building and is found on Craftsman style homes.

Palladian windows: A grouping of three windows, the central being taller and with an arched top. This feature was used in late examples of Queen Anne houses by Miller.

pediment: The triangular upper part of the facade of a building in the Classical style and characterized by a low roof angle.

rafter tails: The lower ends of the rafters (roof framing) that have been left exposed to give a rustic appearance, commonly seen in Craftsman Bungalows.

scrollwork: Decorative trim generated on a scroll-saw (jigsaw), such as brackets, balusters, or gable ornaments, common on Victorian houses

sidelights: A narrow row of windows along both sides of a front doorway, and maybe above the transom as well. This feature is seen in Colonial Revival houses.

spindlework: Fancy Victorian trim generated on a lathe, including columns and balusters.

sunburst ornamentation: Gable ornament with a radiating pattern.

trim: Plain board used to cover the ends of clapboard siding at the edge or top of the wall.

vernacular: Ordinary or lacking in style or pretension.

wraparound porch: A porch extending along at least two sides of a house, and which may have rounded corners, or incorporate a pediment over the front entrance. Miller used wraparound porches on Queen Anne homes.

Table 2
Hallmarks of Style as Interpreted by John Campbell Miller

Queen Anne--Spindlework Type (1880-1910)
- Steep hipped roof with lower cross gables and other roof complexities
- Cutaway bay windows with brackets supporting roof corners, often with tower-like effect
- Wrap-around porches, often curved, with brackets, turned columns, and balusters
- Gingerbread ornamentation used on brackets and gable trim

Queen Anne--Free Classic Type (1890-1910)
- General building plan as above but with less ornamental woodwork
- Porches with Doric columns, and gables with Palladian windows

Shingle (1880-1910)
- Gambrel roof with cross gables
- Spindle-work on wide porches, as in Queen Anne style

Richardsonian Romanesque (1880-1900)
- Hipped roof with hipped dormers, square tower
- Round topped arch over door and masonry (brick) walls, very massive effect

Folk Victorian (1870-1910)
- Side-gabled with cornice-line brackets
- Spindle-work porch detailing with jigsaw-cut trim, bay windows

Colonial Revival (1880-1955)
- Side-gabled roof with symmetrical façade and massive cornices
- Front door with multiple pane windows on the side and above the transom

Prairie (1900-1920)
- Four-square with low pitched roof, usually hipped with hipped dormers
- Overhanging eaves, boxed in and massive, square porch supports

Craftsman (1905-1930)
- Low-pitched, side-gabled roof with wide unenclosed eave overhang and hipped dormers
- Exposed rafter tails and decorative braces under gables
- Windows abundant, often in groups of two or three
- Porches wide, supported by tapered square columns

Vernacular
- Plain unadorned buildings seen mainly with churches and stores

2

Greenville and West Along the Indian Creek Valley

The Greenville area was settled early because the first settlers simply followed an existing Indian road and selected farm sites along the rich alluvial bottom land in the early 1770s. Indian Creek and tributaries were suitable for mill sites and local limestone caves yielded saltpeter, a key ingredient of gunpowder.[6] The place was called Indian Creek in early times and the local center of the settlement was initially Cooks Fort, built in 1774 on the Valentine Cook property. This was intended as a defense against possible Indian attacks during Lord Dunmore's War, but was used through the American Revolution. Soon after, Cooks Mill was built at the point where Laurel Creek joins Indian Creek, and, eventually, a Post Office was established at the mill in 1831.[7] A village was laid out in 1846 on a promontory just east of the Cook lands and named Centreville. This was on the land of Robert and Rachel Shanklin and most of the house lots were quickly snapped up, and stores and churches were established.

The name Centreville was replaced by Greenville in 1890, about the time Miller began work in Monroe County. He started a new wave of building and several of his houses (Nos. 3-7) were located in the center of the town. These represent a variety of styles and No. 8 is a magnificent farm just west on Ellison's Ridge Road. Two others are west of Greenville (Nos. 9A, 10) on State Route 122 while one (No. 9) was near Wayside, but was destroyed by fire. Descriptions and pictures of these buildings are found on the following pages.

3. ROBERT S. DUNLAP: This structure was built in the Folk Victorian style with large bay windows, curved cornice brackets, and a simple, practical roof line. The interior features floor-to-ceiling windows, a built-in china cabinet, and stairway newel posts with concentric circle embellishments. A two-story addition was made to the rear of the house as were the porch and columns around the entire façade and left side. In its long life, the exterior has been different colors. Recently, the home has been light blue and currently is pale yellow.

Built in 1899, the house was first located on Lot 17 on Main Street in Greenville. Issac Newton "Ike" Ballard (1864-1960) and Kate May Walkup Ballard (1864-1944) were early owners.[8] Ike Ballard was a merchant, Indian Creek postmaster, and organizer and first president of the Bank of Greenville. Their daughters, Margaret Burnside "Maggie" Ballard (1900-1976), a doctor and historian, and Helen Houston Ballard (1902-1972) were born during the family's residence there.

In 1917, it was sold to Robert "Bert" Smart Dunlap (1869-1926) and Elizabeth Patterson (1880-1972) and was moved across the street to Lot 28 on the corner of Main and South

Dunlap House, 2019. Photo by Becky Crabtree.

streets. They were married in Redlands, California, at the home of her sister, Julia Patterson Hunt. The couple met in about 1895 and promised to marry after the death of Elizabeth's father, Marion Patterson. She had made a vow to her father that she would take care of him for the rest of his life. They married a week after his death, nearly 20 years later in 1912, a true love story. Robert and Beth Dunlap had two sons, Marion Addison Dunlap (1914-1986) and Edward Patterson "Pat" Dunlap (1917-2010). Robert died of a stroke in Talcott while riding the train home to Greenville. Rhonda Dortch is the current owner of the home.

*Dunlap House, 1988.
Photo by Irene Greene.*

Dunlap House before it was moved across the street. Small building in the rear was once Sam Garrison's shoe shop where "box toed" boots were made and priced at $7. On the right is the back of Ballard's Store. Prior to 1917. Photo from Caperton Museum, Monroe County West Virginia Historical Society, Ballard photo file.

Dunlap House before it was moved. Prior to 1917. wvhistoryonview.org/catalog/013699. A&M 2537 Ballard Collection. West Virginia and Regional History Collection, West Virginia University Libraries.

Side view of Dunlap House which corresponds to the front of house at earlier location. 2019. Photo by Becky Crabtree.

*Dunlap House interior features during modern renovation:
(L) front room bay and (R) newel posts at the top of stairs, 2019.
Photos by Becky Crabtree.*

*Elizabeth "Libbie" Patterson Dunlap with son, Marion, 1914.
findagrave.com/memorial/5528947/elizabeth-dunlap.
Photo added by Kevin Thomas West.*

4. ISSAC N. BALLARD: This expansive two-story home is located on Lot 17 on Main Street in Greenville. Built in the Folk Victorian style, it has its own stately prestige without the frills of the Queen Anne houses. It does display a large bay window on its front, a side porch, and bracketed cornices. The two-story columns were not part of the original structure.

Issac Newton "Ike" Ballard and Kate May Walkup Ballard were married in 1893 and bought the house in 1917. Their daughter, Dr. Maggie Ballard, wrote, "the family of the bride objected to their marriage on the grounds that Ike was a Republican, a descendant of a Union sympathizer, a Baptist, and last but certainly not the least of the objectionable characteristics – he drove two horses in his buggy and raced through the town in a very reckless manner. In spite of all this, Ike and Mary lived together for more than 50 years and celebrated their golden wedding anniversary by receiving many friends at their home in Greenville."

The home and lot adjoined Ballard's store, Ballard & Thomas, which later became the Ballard, Thomas & Company and still later, Ballard & Arnott when Robert H. Arnott became his business partner. The home formerly belonged to Charles L. Miller of Hinton, West Virginia, and was occupied by A.A. McNeer and family. Today it is owned by Eva May Chandler, who was married to the grandson of Ike and Kate Ballard, son of Helen Houston Clark, Thomas Ballard Chandler.

Issac N. Ballard Home, 1988.
Photo provided by Irene Greene.

CHAPTER TWO

*Issac N. Ballard Home, 2019.
Photo by Becky Crabtree.*

*(L) Issac N. Ballard, date unknown.
(R) Issac N. and K. May Ballard,
date unknown.
Caperton Museum, Monroe County,
West Virginia Historical Society,
Ballard photo file.*

Portrait of Maggie and Helen Ballard, about 1904. wvhistoryonview/catalog/013576. A&M 2537 Ballard Collection. West Virginia and Regional History Collection, West Virginia University Libraries.

Dr. Maggie Ballard, one of the first women to earn a medical degree from the University of Maryland. About 1925. wvhistoryonview/catalog/013810. A&M 2537 Ballard Collection, Udel Bros., Baltimore, Maryland, West Virginia and Regional History Collection, West Virginia University Libraries.

5. ROBERT H. ARNOTT: This Queen Anne style home sits on Lot 39 of Greenville's South Street. It is a one-and-a-half story home, considerably smaller than others of the Queen Anne style homes built by Miller. The front and back of the house appear similar with a single dormer on the left and a shingled gable on the right. The trim on the front is more ornate, with a narrow decorative frieze following the porch roof line, bracketed porch posts, and complex ornamentation in the peaks.

Tom Shanklin was the original owner and may have assisted with construction since it was reported that his initials were cut in the cornice of dormers. Water access was likely from a public fountain in place about 1848. The house was built about 1905.

The owners were Robert "Bub" Handley Arnott (1871-1936) and wife Jane "Janie" Robinson Bittinger (1865-1943). They bought the house in 1907, the year of their marriage. Jane was the daughter of the Rev. M. H. Bittinger (1826-1913), beloved pastor of the Centerville Presbyterian Church in Greenville who served there for more than 50 years beginning in 1855. The reference to a parsonage in the list of Miller houses compiled by his daughter and granddaughter may have been to the Methodist parsonage that possibly stood on this site earlier.

Arnott House, 2019.
Photo by Becky Crabtree.

Arnott purchased an interest in the Ballard & Thomas Store in 1897 after the store had burned and was rebuilt. In the 1910 census, Arnott is listed as a general merchant of retail dry goods. He was commissioned as the 14th postmaster in Greenville in 1914. His Civil Examination reveals that he was an excellent student in arithmetic and accounts (97 percent), but penmanship was poor (73 percent). His handwriting was judged almost illegible. The Arnotts took an extended western tour in 1915, visiting Yellowstone Park, Salt Lake City, and the World's Fair in San Francisco. His business partner, Ike Ballard, covered the post office and mercantile business for several weeks during their absence. In 1919, Jane was employed as a post office clerk.

Other owners include Danny Thompson, Sharon Anderson, and Mary and Jeanie Smith. This charming home has been owned by Howdy and Suzie Henritz since 2000. They chose a tasteful two-tone paint job with white trim and light grey walls.

Paul's pony cart with Paul, Maggie, Roy, Stella, and Ruth Ballard. Arnott house is in the background. About 1912. Caperton Museum, Monroe County, West Virginia Historical Society, Ballard Photos.

Bay in front of Arnott House, 2018. Photo by Becky Crabtree.

"New" store building stands in the corner of Main Street in Greenville. Built 1896. R.H. Arnott, standing. I.N. Ballard, seated. Note "Post Office" sign on post. Caperton Museum, Monroe County, West Virginia Historical Society, Ballard

Ballard and Arnott Store. Date Unknown. wvhistoryonview/catalog/013608. A&M 2537 Ballard Collection, West Virginia and Regional History Collection, West Virginia University Libraries.

6. LONG STORE: The two-story store building was located in Greenville on State Route 122 and was probably built about 1915. The store was plain-looking, front-gabled with a small round window in the gable. There were living quarters on the second floor and the business was on the ground level. The building is nearly identical to another store in Greenville, Ballard & Arnott Mercantile.

Once owned and operated by Frank Maddy as Maddy's Store, it later became the General Store, and after that, Long's Store. According to an account of Marshalene Pence Evans, whose parents, Forest D. and Eva Mae Harvey Pence, owned and ran the business during the 1940s, "At the rear of the store was a large pot-bellied Warm Morning stove with chairs, benches, and maybe a nail keg or two surrounding it. Every night several men in town would gather round this stove to 'loaf.' There was no self-service in the store as we are familiar with today. Customers would stand at a counter and read out their list of groceries. Mom or Dad would run all over the store and bring the items back to the counter. Other than groceries they also sold dry goods. These were items such as dress and quilt materials, sewing supplies, linens, a few gift items and toys, some clothing and shoes and some hardware items. On the dry goods side of the store there were shelves that reached all the way to the ceiling. In order to have access to them there was a tall ladder that was hooked to the ceiling and had rollers on the bottom. It could be moved from one end of the shelves to the other. Besides being essential to reach the upper shelves, it was also my private place to pull my teeth when they needed to come out. I would climb to the very top, sit there for a while contemplating just how I was going to accomplish this gruesome task.

Long Store, 1988. Photo provided by Irene Greene.

They also stocked a small amount of medicines. Some that I remember are paregoric (for baby teething and pain), sweet oil (for earaches), flour sulphur (for sore throats), Porter's Liniment Salve (for cuts and sores). ... They also sold fresh fish which came in a large wooden barrel which smelled horrible. Dried beans were located in bulk behind the counter. These were scooped out, weighed, placed in a 'poke' and tied with twine string. There was a Texaco gas pump out front at the wooden porch and a kerosene tank out back. Also, in the back room were many different large sacks of grain and feed for chickens, cows, hogs, etc. My mother and others used the sacks to make clothing."[9]

Reba Saunders Long (1926-2021) confirmed Marshalene's description of the store's interior. Her husband, Orville Milton "Shorty" Long (1925-2007) and his two brothers, Otis (1919-1992) and Allen (1921-1978), jointly owned the store until it was torn down in the early 1990s.

7. JOHN FRANK MADDY: This two-story Prairie style home sat behind the Maddy Store in Greenville on State Route 122. Built in 1901, the home is a Four-Square type with a low-pitched roof which is hipped with overhanging eaves and has cornice-lined brackets. It also has a tower, more a trademark of Queen Anne houses than Prairie style residences. Massive square porch supports and triple windows complete the features of the large home.

Frank Maddy's House, front view, 2019. Photo by Becky Crabtree.

John Frank Maddy (1880-1935) married Zula Gertrude Shirey (1883-1962) in 1907. The Maddys had two daughters, Anna Rebecca Collins (1908-2001) and Ruth Elinor born in 1910 who died at 9 months old.

Frank Maddy, as he was known, graduated from Dunsmore Business College in 1898. On his draft card in 1918, his profession was listed as merchant. His obituary in the Staunton (Virginia) News-Leader stated, "Mr. Maddy was a merchant and farmer; a man held in the highest esteem by everyone with whom he was acquainted."

The house was owned later by Ralph Monroe (1923-2005) and Ruby Lee Mann Lawhorn (1927-1990) for nearly 50 years. It is now owned by Erica and Mike Smith; their son, Brandon, and his family are current residents.

Frank Maddy's House, side view, 2019. Photo by Becky Crabtree.

8. JOHN R. JOHNSON: This grand 1907 Queen Anne home located just outside Greenville across Indian Creek has a wide porch that extends across the entire front, rounding the left side and angling the corner to the right to extend partially around both sides of the home. The large porch roof is supported by Doric columns. The third-floor windows include two sets of Palladian windows and a half-circle window. A hipped roof tops four gables facing in three directions and decorative treatments adorn the windows.

Inside, stairs are bordered with slender curved balusters and an impressive newel post topped with an urn-shaped cap which can be found in the 1910 Sears Builders Catalog. The heavy wooden front door is pictured in the same catalog. It sports a large beveled oval glass inset framed with elaborate scrollwork. The second-floor landing/hallway is large enough for a sitting room. The interior doors feature stenciled grain patterns, a common practice at the time. A built-in oak china cabinet and columned mantle are among the beautiful accessories of the era along with the original oak sliding doors between the front rooms which are still in place. The home was wired for electricity and the plaster ceilings were replaced with sheetrock and insulated. When the fireplace millwork was removed for wiring the wall, "Sears 1907" was found stamped on the back. No exterior weatherboards have been replaced and the interior trim was made of hemlock, a softer wood, so it could be taken off and put back up easily and never had termites, according to the current owner. There is a back stairway to an upstairs room that may have been for the live-in help.

The house was built for John Robert "Jack" Johnson (1870-1944) who patterned it after the house in Willow Bend, West Virginia, where he was born, according to his daughter, Mary Kathleen "Thummie" Johnson Dunn, (1920-2016). It was known as Cook's Fort Farm.

She wrote that her father was well-respected and seemed to always make people laugh. Among his many occupations, she reported, were Monroe County teacher, sheriff, assessor, county commissioner, livestock and machinery salesman, and owner of Cooks Mill, then called Greenville Roller Mills. The history of the mill is detailed at this website: Cooks Old Mill at Greenville, West Virginia (cooksoldmill.com). Jack was married twice, first, in 1897, to Georgia Young (1873-1915). They had six children: William Robert Johnson (1899-1974), Glenna Lucille Cody (1904-1966), Alma Gertrude Grey Morgan Fischmann (1905-1992), John Edwin (1907-1976), Anna Ethel Mann (1909-2003), and Sarah Elizabeth Sally Phipps (1912-1975). In 1918, he married Mattie Reeves Brown (1895-1968) with whom he had two children, "Thummie" and Jack Jr. "Eddie" (1929-?). When Johnson died, he left the house to his two children from the second marriage.

The house was purchased by Layman Thomas from the Johnson heirs, including "Thummie." The current residents are Layman and Laurie Thomas. They were married in the front parlor.

Johnson House, front view, note Palladian windows, 2019. Photo by Becky Crabtree.

Johnson House, side view, 2019. Photo by Becky Crabtree.

*Interior features of the Jack Johnson House: Built-in cabinet and newel post and stairs, 2018.
Photos by Becky Crabtree.*

*Intricate front door at Jack Johnson's House, 2018.
Photo by Becky Crabtree.*

*Georgia Young Johnson and John Robert "Jack" Johnson, date unknown.
Photos from Find A Grave.*

Jack Johnson and children at their home.
Left to right: Gertrude, Eddie, Lucille, Grandpa Jack, Sally,
and Ethel, who the family called Sis. About 1918.
Photo provided by Jack Johnson's granddaughter, Jennie Phipps.

9. ROBERT E. RINER: This large two-story Queen Anne style home was built on a farm northeast of Wayside, West Virginia. The residence was surrounded by a white board fence, numerous outbuildings, and a large barn set on a knoll just outside the backyard. It features the standard elements of the style: a picturesque front porch with turned posts and decorative brackets, ornamentation in the peak of the front gable, a hipped roof, and gables facing in multiple directions. Judging from the Victorian features, this house was likely built prior to 1906.

It burned in the late 1900s. Robert E. Riner (1881-1963) married Ethel Boon (1882-1972) in 1914. They lived in this home, but it was likely built by Riner's parents, William C. Riner (1820-1895) and Sarah H. Green (1848-1892).

(Note: William Riner's brother, John Thompson Riner, also had a home built by John Campbell Miller.)

Riner House, 1988. Photo provided by Irene Greene.

9A. MARY JANE PENCE: This Colonial Revival style structure was remodeled extensively by Miller prior to 1894. Hewn logs can still be found under the kitchen and large logs remain underneath the porch. The original rear of the house was torn down in 1945. Located at 7332 Greenville Road, the house features a symmetrical facade, pediment-like gables, heavy cornices, and sidelights around the facade doors on two levels. The front doors, one upstairs and one downstairs, both opening to similar porches, are identical. The interior stairs have a curving rail and simple, slender spindles. Wide, unadorned fireplace facings and woodwork are found throughout the home. Years ago, the house was painted white with dark shutters. Today, the color remains but the shutters are no longer in place.

Local historian Otis Pence said that Richard Franklin Neel owned 1,700 acres along Indian Creek and willed it all to his daughter, Mary Jane Neel (1832-1920). She married Lewis Alexander Pence (1832-1900) in 1858 and their children were Horatia Gertrude (1859-1948), Dewey E. Pence (1861-1936), whose nearby home is described later, Mary Victoria (1865-?), and Nannie J. (1869-1899), who married Dr. James Boon in 1884.

Mary Jane Pence lived in the house and in 1894 advertised it in a summer home brochure published by the Monroe Watchman: "Mrs. Mary J Pence, Greenville W.Va., is prepared to take care of 20 boarders for the Summer. Her large and handsome residence is in one of the loveliest portions of the Indian Creek Valley. Nearby is a mineral spring the water of which has been analyzed and found to be identical with the waters of Red Sulphur Springs, 6 miles distant. Terms moderate. Station, Lowell, C&O Railway, 10 miles distant."

The heirs of Lewis Pence sold the home in 1945. The most recent resident of the home, Otis Pence, was a distant relative of Mary Jane Pence. Sadly, Pence passed away during the writing of this book as a result of burns from an accident while burning brush near the house.

Mary Jane Pence House, side view, 1988. Photo provided by Irene Greene.

Mary Jane Pence House: the front door from the inside, an example of side lights and transom light, 2018.
Stair rails, 2019.
Photos by Becky Crabtree.

Mary Jane Pence House, front view, 2020. Photo by Becky Crabtree.

10. GEORGE P. YOUNG: Built prior to 1900, this home is an example of Queen Anne style with a steep hipped roof and gables facing in different directions. It has a front porch that wraps around the left side and gingerbread trim decorates the peaks of gables. The porch supports are bracketed with scrollwork. The house is eye-catching, currently painted light brown with white trim. It is located just off State Route 122 about three miles west of Greenville.

It is likely the Youngs, George P. Young (1837-1908) and Nancy "Nannie" Peck Young (1843-?), married in 1872, were the original owners, and lived there with daughters Mary Francis and Georgia. She was married to John Robert Johnson (their home was described earlier) until her death in 1915.

The following story was told about George Young by Charles B. Dunlap:
"Old George Young was a Civil War veteran who lived alone in the Young's family house where Hans Creek empties into Indian Creek. When he was real old, he took a turn of corn over to the mill at Greenville and, after he left it at the mill, went up to Bub Arnott's store in Greenville where there were usually a few loafers sitting on the front

porch spitting at flies. George had lived alone for a long time and had gotten out of the habit of talking. He sat there in silence and listened to the other men boasting about their exploits. The talk turned to throwing stones and one of them told how he had killed himself a mess of frogs by throwing stones in a swampy place in Indian Creek near Greenville. Another man topped this one. He claimed that he was up in the weeds without his rifle and saw some squirrels. He killed three of them by throwing rocks and made himself a good supper. There was a long silence and then old George spoke for the first time, "When I was coming down the Indian Creek road this evening with a turn of corn thinking about nothing, I seen a little rabbit setting on the side of the road. So, I got down off my mule and I picked up a rock and I throwed it at him (Long pause.) Sure enough, I missed him."

The house has been owned by Craig Newkirk, Jennifer Lowry, and is now occupied by current owners, James and Deborah Ashley.

Young House, view from right, 2019. Photo by Becky Crabtree.

CHAPTER TWO 43

Young House, view from left, 2019. Photo by Becky Crabtree.

3

The Lower Hans Creek Valley

Hans Creek is a left tributary of Indian Creek and was settled prior to the American Revolution. The lower part of the valley is 4½ miles long and about a quarter mile wide, just wide enough to accommodate some beautiful farms on both sides of County Route 25. In fact, a sign at the lower end says "Welcome, Hans Creek Valley." Schools and a church anchor a small community together with the Larew Spring, a sulphur spring, and "a large and comfortable country residence" developed there to put up visitors in the 19th century. Otherwise, this valley is farmland and was named for an early hunter, John Hand, or Hance, in Revolutionary times. Notable is the Ellison Farm which was established in 1774 and is still farmed by the same family. At one time, the Ellison family operated a grist and sawmill.

John Campbell Miller lived on a side valley of Hans Creek called Wesley Holler early on. Wesley Holler was located between the communities of Red Sulphur Springs and Hans Creek, just below the top of Kibble Hill. It was also known as Sam Miller Holler and Sugar Run, the name of the stream that flows through it. There was a settlement there in the late 1800s that consisted of at least five houses with the usual barns, corn cribs, and other agricultural structures.

Sam Miller had a big house at the head of the hollow and his son Arthur Dean Miller lived there. Benjamin and Safronia Wesley and family lived there. John

Campbell and Lillie Miller and their children lived there, too. In time, Fred and Florence Miller Wesley made a home with their girls, Glenna, Lillie, and Irene. John Campbell Miller made his home here before he left the area and when he came back to visit his daughter, this is where he returned. Today, no house, no outline of a house's foundation, not even a pile of chimney stones can be found to tell the story of this era in this place. All that can be found is a wide valley of lush pasture between two mountains.

Most of the buildings in Hans Creek were his creations. Sadly, some of the big old Queen Anne farmhouses have been lost. Buildings by Miller are Nos. 11-18, and 57-58 and include the Hans Creek Church.

11. DEWEY E. PENCE: This exquisite Queen Anne style home, built in 1906, features exterior cutaway gables supported by brackets and crowned by gable ornaments in full Victorian regalia. The interior features a floating landing, an oval window, several curved interior walls, and two sets of bay windows giving views of the lush Hans Creek Valley to the north and to the south. The front door glass is embellished with decorative floral and cherub patterns and there is a transom above each interior door. Other nods to the era include horsehair in the plaster and closets too narrow for today's coat hangers.

Dewey Edwin Pence (1861-1936) and Ella Marietta Arnot Pence (1861-1952) were married in 1875 and were the original owners of this classic home. Dewey was the son of Mary Jane and Louis Pence. He was an elder in the Centerfield Presbyterian Church and worked for 30 years at the Greenville Telephone Company. His obituary stated, "Early on in life, he chose the way of sobriety and useful living." Before marriage, he "made a tour of several months through a number of the western states seeking a future home. Finding no place more pleasing, he returned to cast his lot among the friends of his childhood." He married Ella, daughter of Elisha and Ruth Arnot, in 1885. They celebrated their golden wedding anniversary the year before he died. They raised two daughters, Maggie Gray Pence and Grace Glenna Pence Braden.

The house has also been the home of the Kuhns, Warren and Judy Kuhn Ellison (their daughter's wedding was held here), the Estills, and the Vetters. The land has been farmed for at least the last 240 years; the original farm was surveyed in 1774 and contained 363 acres. It is now occupied by former Wyoming County, West Virginia, assistant superintendent of schools, James McGrady, who actively operates the adjoining cattle farm from his home.

Dewey Pence House, about 1910. Photo provided by James McGrady.

Dewey Pence House, side view, 2018. Photo by Becky Crabtree.

Dewey Pence House front view, 2018. Photo by Becky Crabtree.

Trim on front gable of Dewey Pence House. Some of the "gingerbread" trim was hinged to fit a variety of angles in the peaks of the gables. 2018. Photo by Becky Crabtree.

*Warren and Judy Ellison with daughter, Barbara Level,
in front of bay window of Dewey Pence House, about 1944.
Photo provided by James McGrady with permission of Barbara Level.*

12. ADDISON DUNLAP: The brother of Addison Dunlap, James A. Dunlap (1799-1843) was the first to move to Hans Creek.[10] He married Frances McElheney in 1831 and had a store at Red Sulphur Springs with Andrew Beirne by 1832, so chances are that the brick part of this home was built about that time. The initial brick house was a cross-gabled, early Classical Revival Style building with a formal, two-story porch supported by Doric columns. The brick structure now forms the right side of the current building. The bricks were made from clay found east of the vegetable garden and fired on the place. The mortar was also made there and the inside walls were plastered, which was pretty fancy for the era. The plaster was mixed with hair, most of it looking like pig bristles, to help it hold together. The roof was made of walnut shingles, each fitted individually, and lasting just short of a hundred years.[11] James died early. He owned six enslaved people when he died; he left four to his wife and one, a girl, to his younger brother Addison (1801-1870) who inherited the house with another brother, Alexander. Alexander died in 1853, leaving the house to Addison.

Addison married his second wife, Clara Petrie Dunlap (1804-1884) in 1834 and they moved into the house in 1844. Addison was a prominent citizen and bought the Red Sulphur Springs resort in 1843 together with brothers Thomas and Isaac Campbell for $25,000. He also owned a store in Red Sulphur with his brother Alexander. At one point he was president of the Red Sulphur and Blue Sulphur Springs Turnpike.[12]

Addison and Clara had five children, James, Charles H., Addison, Jane A., and Harriet Petrie. Eventually, ownership of the homestead was passed on to Charles (1839-

1904) who married Martha Smart Bates in 1862. The third generation of Dunlaps to occupy the house was William P. (1868-1944) and Elsie Nason (1867-1941), brother and sister. Their nephew, Charles, born about 1910, visited there as a child and wrote a long manuscript about his experiences. This was the period in which the Miller addition was put on, about 1917. In a recently discovered manuscript, Charles Dunlap described the construction:

"About 1914 or 1915, Uncle Billie (W. P. Dunlap) and Deedie (Elsie Nason Dunlap), brother and sister who ran the farm during the time I knew it, decided that the combination of the brick house and the log house was not satisfactory so they decided to build a 'frame house.' The log house was jacked up, put on log rollers and moved inch by inch in a direction up the branch to make room for the new house.

"Building the new house was a major undertaking that made a tremendous impression on me as a child of about seven. Most of it was a local operation. Trees were cut and a sawmill was set up about 100 yards up the branch from the old house together with a big shack for curing the lumber. This was a temporary two-story job with a fire on the ground floor and a section above it where the lumber was stacked to dry out in the heat. Stone was dug up locally and also brought in on horse drawn sleds from the stone piles that had accumulated around some of the stony fields of the farm. It was decided to build a cellar under part of the house and this was excavated with shovel and mattock (pronounced maddick) and one-horse dump scoops. Rock was encountered during the excavation and this required some blasting. The blasting holes were drilled by hand, one man holding the drill and turning it while another man hit it with a sledge. A slit was cut in the side of a stick of dynamite with a pocketknife and a black powder fuse like the one on a firecracker was laid in the slit. This was lowered into the hole and the end lighted. Then everyone ran like mad before the explosion. A good stonemason was brought in from outside to build the stone foundation but as far as I know everything else was done locally. While the house was being built, running water was installed for the first time."[13]

This second stage of the home's construction included the wood frame sections of the front and left side of the structure, completed in 1917. The simplistic farmhouse style is impressive for the size, large enough to have two front entrances, one on either side of the lower front porch. Extending the length of this expansive home are both a lower and an upper porch, the second-floor porch edged by nearly 200 spindles. Both porches are supported by turned posts. The third-floor attic boasts double windows on three sides of the home. The house contains pristine hardwood floors; square, flat-topped newel posts; doors with stenciled grain; and a built-in oak china cabinet. Located on Hans Creek Road, the home sits just out of sight of the road on the eastern side of State Route 25.

Several unrelated owners followed through the middle of the 20th century. In the early 1970s, the property was reacquired by a descendant of the Dunlaps, Harriet Petrie Ellison Dobbs, and husband Lee Filmore Dobbs. Harriet was connected through Jane, daughter of the original Addison Dunlap, who had married John Zachariah Ellison also of Hans Creek. (The neighboring Ellison home is described later in the chapter.) The Dobbs modernized the house and their son and daughter, Addison and

Petrie, still own it. For many years, Addison had a successful dairy operation there. The house is currently unoccupied.

*Original brick Addison Dunlap home, built around 1830.
It remains as part of the existing structure.
West Virginia and Regional History Collection, West Virginia University Libraries.*

*Sketch of Dunlap House by Judith Blair, 1979.
Photo provided by Petrie Brown and used with permission of the artist.*

*Wedding reception at the Dunlap House, 1978.
Photo provided by Petrie Brown.*

Side view of Dunlap House, 2019. Photo by Becky Crabtree.

*Built-in cabinet in Dunlap House,
typical of other homes built by John Campbell Miller.
2019. Photo by Becky Crabtree.*

Cabins of enslaved people, about 18 feet square each, which were adapted to other uses after the Civil War: smoke house, chicken house, carpenter shop, ice house, blacksmith shop, ash house (all dismantled in 1964) in front left of Dunlap House, date unknown. Photo provided by Petrie Brown.

54   JOHN CAMPBELL MILLER

13. LETCHER E. MILLER: This Queen Anne style home was built in 1901 on the western side of County Route 25. Located near Greenville in the community known as Hans Creek, it featured a wide porch that extended around two sides, distinctive "sunbeam" ornamentation in the peaks of the gables, and at least one bay window. It was most recently painted all white, but older photographs show dark trim around porch posts and windows. The house is no longer standing. Letcher E. Miller (1860-1937) and Minnie Ballard Miller (1864-1946) were married in 1900 and were the owners. He was a teacher in the late 1800s and then became a farmer. His father was William F. Miller whose father was born in Scotland. The same site was the home of John Henderson and Clara S. Peck Vawter and their 13 children. John was a captain in the Confederate army. Four of their sons also served in the Confederate army. One was killed in the Battle of Seven Pines. George W. Vawter was their youngest son and was 10 years old when the Civil War ended and remembered his brothers, Charles and Lewis, returning home from the war across the Hans Creek bottom pasture. George Vawter's home was built by John Campbell Miller across the creek about a third of a mile from his homeplace. It is described here later.

Letch Miller Place, about 1960.
Photo provided by Clark Humphreys.

CHAPTER THREE   55

*Letch and Lee Miller at Letch's home on Hans Creek, about 1920.
Photo provided by Clark Humphreys.*

14. WILBUR L. BROYLES: This majestic Queen Anne home was built in the Hans Creek community near Greenville on the eastern side of County Route 25. The entire length of the front of the house is wrapped in an inviting first-floor porch that curves around to include the right side. It incorporates a pediment at the front door. Three gables face in three directions and at least two are adorned with "sunburst" patterned trim in the peaks as is the peak of the pediment. The house was painted a light color with porch railings, windows and wall edges painted a darker color.

It was first owned by Wilbur Lee Broyles (1874-1940) and Minnie Pearl Calloway Broyles Frazier (1874-1975). They had six children: Gladys Lynch (1899-2004), Helen Mae Broyles (1900-1988), Otis Christopher (1902-1908), Roy Edwin (1906-1988), Ida Katherine (1908-1994), and Alice Calloway (1914-1987). The home and farm were leased to the Frank Campbell family in 1924, but Broyles was never happy in their new home in Princeton and they eventually moved back. He was of Irish heritage and remembered by granddaughter Roberta Larew Allison as being full of fun. She told a story in which he explained hair licks. "As soon as I was born, they took me out to the barn and let old Jersey lick me!" Another story involved a 400-pound female relative who visited the outhouse and caused it to collapse. It was reported he was not allowed to share the tale if his wife was around. He was also known for giving pet lambs to neighborhood children every spring. According to Allison, her grandmother had him declared insane and tried to sell the farm, but the children stepped in and saved the property. The house has been razed.

In January 2020, Matthew Dobbs, son of Addison Dobbs (co-owner of the Dunlap house) and Laurie Dobbs Thomas (wife of Layman Thomas, who lives in the Jack Johnson house), his wife Samantha, and their two sons moved into their new home built on this site.

*Wilbur Broyles house, date unknown.
Photo provided by Clark Humphreys.*

*Minnie Pearl Calloway Broyles, wife of Wilbur Broyles, 1897.
Photo provided by Gladys Carter.*

CHAPTER THREE   57

Wilbur and Minnie Broyles, at the George Vawter house. They were neighbors and frequent visitors, about 1911. Photo provided by their great-grandson, Robert Larew.

15. GEORGE W. VAWTER: This stately two-story Folk Victorian home is nestled in the valley of Hans Creek at the foot of Kibble Hill, between Ballard and Greenville. A small front porch is supported by bracketed posts and topped with a frieze constructed of repetitive small post turnings. Matching bay windows adorn either side of the front and another is found on the eastern-facing side. Two original porches, upper and lower, ran the length of the western-facing side of the house, but have now been enclosed. Inside, narrow interlocking wormy chestnut boards cover a bedroom wall, a mirrored wooden parlor fireplace mantel, and a built-in china cabinet add to the décor. There are four bedrooms, a dining room, a parlor, and kitchen. The house was located on 150 acres of farmland.

It was built in 1899 by Miller and David Halstead who were hired by George W. Vawter (1855-1934) and Eliza Lively Gwinn (1860-1942). They were married in 1879 and had one daughter, Sarah Josephine Hines (1892-1966). Her daughter, Elizabeth Hines Czompo (1914-2014) wrote "Memories of Hans Creek," which details life at this home. She writes, "There was a front stairway and a back stairway. The front stairway was made from a walnut log taken from the home of my grandfather's grandfather – just across the road. The two-story add-on at the back of the house had walls filled with sawdust to make a freeze-proof structure. The second-floor part was the place where my grandmother kept a sugar barrel, smoked meat, and some home canned food. My grandmother often said, 'I haven't seen the bottom of that sugar barrel since World War I!' That was true. During World War I she had run out of sugar … and never let that happen again."

The house was recently purchased by Robert Larew and Michael Lentz.

George Vawter House, 1988. Photo provided by Irene Greene.

George Vawter House, 2019. Photo by Becky Crabtree.

CHAPTER THREE 59

*Doll cradle made by John C. Campbell for George Vawter's daughter, Josephine, when he built the house, 1899.
Photo provided by Robert Larew.*

*Robert G. Vawter in the front yard, about 1905.
Photo provided by Robert Larew.*

The Vawter family on their front porch. The woman nearest the camera is Bessie Gwinn, Eliza Vawter's sister. Behind her is her niece and nearby are her two young girls. The Vawter family that built the house are in the upper right side of the photograph. Eliza and George are seated in the rear and their children, Robert and Josephine are seated in front, about 1910. Photo provided by Robert Larew.

George Vawter (with beard), Eliza to his left, Robert Larew, young girl who is associated with Eliza's sister, Bessie Gwinn, who is seated closest to the camera, about 1918. Photo provided by Robert Larew, grandson of Robert Larew in the photo.

Interior features of the Vawter house: fireplace and built-in cabinet, 2019. Photos by Becky Crabtree.

16. HANS CREEK CHURCH: This vernacular style church was built in Hans Creek in 1912 by Miller and two helpers. The small church features a steeple, belfry, and covered entrance with double doors. The tall windows along the sides have pointed angular tops, a nod to Gothic tradition.

A stranger to Hans Creek, Dan Devere, was walking by and noticed the church needed painting. He was hired and borrowed a set of old clothes to do the job, according to Elizabeth Czompo along with information about the first weddings held there. Her parents, Josephine Vawter and Oat Hines were the first to be married in the church on June 26, 1913, with roses for decoration. The second couple to be married was Gladys Broyles and Robert Larew on September 10, 1919, with goldenrod and Queen Anne's lace on display.[14]

Hans Creek Church, front view, 2020. Photo by Becky Crabtree.

Hans Creek Church, side view, 2020. Photo by Becky Crabtree.

17. CHARLES L. ELLISON: Highlights of this Craftsman cottage include windows in groups of three, a low-pitched roof supported by brackets, and a wide front porch. The use of natural materials is evident in the stacked stone porch posts and dark-stained wooden trim.

Charles Alexander Ellison (1883-1919) and wife, Frances Bailey Waters Ellison (1888-1930), may have had it built in 1912. It is known locally as the "Mill House" and is used as a summer home and a venue for family events. Frances Ellison Hendrick owned it for many years and came from Florida to spend summers in the mountains. The current owners are Barbara Ellison Level and her siblings.

Charlie Ellison House, front view, 1988. Photo provided by Irene Greene.

Charlie Ellison House, side view, 2020. Photo by Becky Crabtree.

18. ADDISON D. ELLISON: This sprawling two-story farmhouse was originally built in 1873 by Jesse and Zachariah Ellison then remodeled extensively by John Campbell Miller in 1913. The land on which this house sits has a long history with the Ellison family.

In 1771, James Ellison (1735-1791) and his wife Anne English Ellison brought their seven children to Hans Creek Valley and cleared land. In 1774 they received a land patent for 82 acres. James left the farm to their son John who died in 1845 and he left it to his son Jesse.[15] Jesse married Alpha Broyles and built a two-story log house. (See photo "View of the early Ellison home," above.) Alpha wove wool and linen in a downstairs room, carding and spinning the fleeces then weaving coverlets and fabric for other needs. Jesse farmed and operated a grist and sawmill. It is told that Alpha saved the farm with income from her weaving. Their son, John Zachariah (1840-1934), was said to have grown up in "hard times." Zack left to fight with the Confederate army and participated in several battles. He surrendered his arms at Appomattox with Robert E. Lee's troops and walked home. He later said that he had been fighting for a wrong cause. Upon his return, he went to Pittsburgh's Iron City Commercial College and completed a course in accounting. While he was gone, his father, Jesse, cut down trees for a new house for his son. Zack returned, helped build the house, and took over the operation of the mill.

The house was a large two-story clapboard home built with walnut logs cured in the mill dam. The middle of the house had a large stone chimney with four fireplaces. The kitchen was behind the house and had its own fireplace and there was a spring house near the kitchen for cooling dairy products.

Alpha died soon after the house was completed and Jesse died two years later, just two months before Zack married Harriet Petrie Dunlap (1846-1911) from a neighboring farm. (The Addison Dunlap house is detailed earlier in this chapter.) She attended Hollins Institute for Women at Lynchburg, Virginia. Zack and Harriet had four children, three sons and a daughter. Their son, Addison Dunlap Ellison (1881-1975), studied agriculture at West Virginia University and returned to the farm in 1905. He married Emma Catherine Kyle (1883-1968) of Falling Springs, Virginia, in 1907 and brought her to his parent's home. His mother, Harriet, died in 1911.

Addison and Emma's family grew quickly. To accommodate their growing family, the house was enlarged in 1913. Miller likely worked with/for the Ellison men on this renovation. (See photo, page 67: "Beginning addition to J.Z. Ellison home.")

"Addison enlarged the house with a wood-burning range and water piped in from a spring. A new basement contained a laundry, fruit storage rooms, and a furnace built to hold the large copper and iron kettles used to heat water, cook food for preserving, and to make soap and lard. A dumbwaiter carried supplies to and from the main floor. The number of bedrooms were increased to seven, a double back porch, 60 feet long, was added, and the front porch was changed.[16] At that time, a bathroom was also added. The "L" shaped home has a corresponding "L" shaped porch supported by rounded columns.

Zack died at age 93 in 1934 and, like those before him, left the farm to the son who returned, in this case, Addison Dunlap Ellison. He left the mill to a grandson, John

Zachariah, known as "Zack the Second."

The farm was passed from Addison and Emma Catherine to their son, Richard Warren Ellison (1924-2019) and his wife, Juliet "Judy" Ellen Kuhn Ellison (b. 1925), who made their home here for many years. (See their photo with Dewey E. Pence, House No. 11 earlier in this chapter.)

Warren's obituary stated: "The Ellison Farm was recognized as having been in the same family since the birth of the Constitution of the United States, handed down directly from father to son during that time. Warren was the sixth-generation farm owner. He, along with his son Bert, have owned and operated the family farm on Hans Creek, West Virginia, that was designated a 'Bicentennial Farm' in 1988.'" Warren and Judy's son Bert and his wife, Paula Ellison, are current residents.

The story behind the story: It is rare that details of a family and a farm are kept intact for very long. The Ellison family's story came to life in an article written by Helen Steele Ellison and George Parkinson in 1980 based on the discovery of a box of Harriet's letters. She died in 1911 and left a treasure trove of history that lay undiscovered for the next six decades. She had kept 400 letters, bound together in groups with shoelaces and corset strings, on a top shelf. They were discovered in a storage room after Addison's death in 1975. Along with other letters found by the family, these documents provided details of a rich history of a family and its farm.

View of the early Ellison home, a split log structure with a large flat rock chimney. John Zachariah Ellison was born there.
wvhistoryonview.org/catalog/014091. A&M 2484. On loan from Warren Ellison. West Virginia and Regional History Collection, West Virginia University Libraries.

*John Zachariah Ellison's house, built in 1873.
wvhistoryonview.org/catalog/013925. A&M 2484.
Acquired from Warren Ellison.
West Virginia and Regional History Collection, West Virginia University Libraries.*

*Clara Measimore standing in front of the house of her father, J.Z. Ellison.
wvhistoryonview.org/catalog/028155. A&M 2484. On loan from Warren Ellison.
West Virginia and Regional History Collection, West Virginia University Libraries.*

Beginning addition to J.Z. Ellison home. Jesse Ellison house in background, 1913. wvhistoryonview.org/catalog/028148. A&M 2484. On loan from Warren Ellison. West Virginia and Regional History Collection, West VirginiaUniversity Libraries.

Addison Ellison house, 1988. Photo provided by Irene Greene.

Portrait of John Zachariah Ellison (1840-1934). Born in Jesse Ellison House, member of the Ellison-Dunlap family and served in the Confederate Army, Lowry's Battery (also called "Centerville Rifles"), during the Civil War, 1905. wvhistoryonview.org/catalog/028123. A&M 2484. Acquired from Warren Ellison. West Virginia and Regional History Collection, West Virginia University Libraries.

A portrait of Harriet Ellison, the daughter of Clara E. (Petrie) Dunlap and Addison Dunlap and the wife of J.Z. Ellison, 1879. wvhistoryonview.org/catalog/028150. A&M 2484. On loan from Warren Ellison. West Virginia and Regional History Collection, West Virginia University Libraries.

CHAPTER THREE 69

A. D. Ellison Sr. Plowing the Garden, Hans Creek, W. Va. Log barn in right background was built by Jesse Ellison sometime prior to 1835. Ca. 1950. wvhistoryonview.org/catalog/033612. West Virginia and Regional History Collection, West Virginia University Libraries.

[Left] Portrait of Addison Ellison. The Friend Studio, 221 Pleasant St., Morgantown, processed the original. ca. 1900. wvhistoryonview.org/catalog/028145. A&M 2484. On loan from Warren Ellison. West Virginia and Regional History Collection, West Virginia University Libraries.
[Right] Portrait of A.D. Ellison, Labor Day 1975. wvhistoryonview.org/catalog/028138. A&M 2484. On loan from Warren Ellison. West Virginia and Regional History Collection, West Virginia University Libraries.

70 JOHN CAMPBELL MILLER

57. FRED WESLEY: This traditional two-story "L-shaped" farmhouse, probably built in the 1870s, once had two stone chimneys and unremarkable lines and window placements. Notable Victorian modifications were made by Miller after purchasing it in 1900: a wrap-around front porch with a center pediment and twin bay windows were built on the front ground level, one in the front room and one in the parlor. He added a double-decker back porch with a set of outside stairs, a kitchen constructed in the rear, and a dining room. He also built a shop where he and daughter Florence made furniture.

Miller married Lillie Belle Miller in 1890. They had seven children: Ray Saleska (1891-1978), an inventor who built the first high-speed Army tank, was recognized for inventing a grenade launcher, and improved the pulleys on military parachutes; infant Bessie Belle (1895-1896); Florence Mary Miller Wesley (1895-1983); George Dewey (1898-1973), owner of Dewey Miller Motors in Huntington and principal owner of the Huntington Airport Inc.; John Clyde (1900-1977); Dorsey Gordon (1904-1987) postmaster in Peterstown; and Katheryn Virginia Miller Dillon (1908-1970). After Lillie's death in 1922, John sold the house to his daughter Florence and her husband, bought a new Model T Ford, and moved to a son's home in Huntington. His house-building days were over and he spent the next 35 years of his life with smaller carpentry projects. Fred Wesley and wife, Florence, moved into the home and lived there for many years.

*The old John C. Miller homeplace, 1944.
Photo provided by Clark Humphreys.*

CHAPTER THREE 71

*A gathering at the Miller homeplace, date unknown.
Photo provided by Clark Humphreys.*

*Miller homeplace showing rear addition, date unknown.
Photo provided by Clark Humphreys.*

Miller home, 1988. Photo provided by Irene Greene.

Miller home, date unknown.
Photo provided by Irene Greene.

*Miller/Wesley Farm, date unknown.
Photo provided by Irene Greene.*

*[Left] Fred Wesley on front porch of his home on Hans Creek, date unknown.
Photo provided by grandson, Johnny Greene.
[Right] Florence Miller and Fred Wesley, in front yard of home, date unknown.
Photo provided by Clark Humphreys.*

58. JOHN C. MILLER: This modest home, a traditional mountain cabin with a front porch, had a two-story addition in more recent times. It was the home of Benjamin Franklin Wesley (1845-1917) and wife Saphronia E. Houchins Wesley (1863-1944). They were married in 1896 after the murder of Wesley's first wife Martha Jane Skaggs Wesley (1845-1892) and three of their children in Wyoming County, West Virginia. Saphronia and Benjamin had a son, Fred Johnson Wesley (1896-1974), who married Florence Miller, John Campbell Miller's daughter, in 1918. They had three daughters, Glenna Lee (1919-1931), Irene Greene (1921-2016), who compiled the photos used in this collection with her mother's help, and Lillie Katherine Humphreys (1923-2018), whose home is described in another entry.

After Saphronia moved in with Fred and Florence in the 1930s, Calvin Scotland Whitten (1875-1955) and son, Burl, lived in the house until Cal's death.

The old John Miller home, a modest cabin, located in Wesley Hollow. Grandma Fronie lived there. Photo provided by Clark Humphreys.

CHAPTER THREE 75

*The old John Miller home in the background with farm outbuildings surrounding it.
Photo provided by Clark Humphreys.*

*On the left, a more modern view of the home with a two-story yellow addition.
Photo provided by Clark Humphreys.*

Wesley Family photo, Fred Wesley front and center, his mother, Sephronia Wesley, directly behind him. Photo provided by Clark Humphreys.

4

Orchard and Pine Grove Road

This northwest trending ridge road follows the west side of Hans Creek Valley with elevations ranging above 2,100 feet and crosses the county from Lindside to Red Sulphur Springs. It is roughly 500 feet above the valley floor and affords breath-taking views in several directions. The high ground is due to a resistant and level sandstone bed 35 to 85 feet thick called the Stony Gap Sandstone. Apparently, the sandstone is porous enough to hold water as reservoirs and lovely farms are found along here. Indian artifacts are common here and it seems likely that this ridge may have been farmed in prehistoric times. It has been noted that the earliest settlers preferred the valleys for their farms, however.

John Campbell Miller built several farmhouses (Nos. 19-24) along County Route 27 which runs along the ridgeline, an area adjacent to Wesley Hollow where he lived. Many have disappeared over the years, including the Orchard Store (No. 22) and the Ryan's Craftsman Cottage (No. 2), although the Plunk Miller House (No. 23), which we classify in the Shingle style, is a striking exception.

2. JOHN R. RYAN: This home exhibits a wide wrap-around porch supported by double columns on a pedestal, the tapered square columns of the Craftsman Cottage style. A low-pitched roof and abundant windows complete the traditional design.

This is said to be the last house Miller built, in about 1922. It was located just over the top of Kibble Hill between Red Sulphur Springs and Hans Creek. The original owner was John Richard "Johnny" Ryan (1851-1933), a farmer whose father immigrated from Ireland, and his wife, Martha Ellen Mann (1853-1926), who was an invalid for the last 30 years of her life. They raised seven children: Rosetta M., Prince Edward, Wilbur L., Henry A., Emma Bell, Norman, and Mabel Lura Freshour. The house was destroyed by fire.

Front view of the last house John Campbell Miller built, located at the top of Kibble Hill, about 1980. Photo provided by Clark Humphreys.

19. DORSE E. LOWE: Located at the top of Kibble Hill between Ballard and Hans Creek, this charming cottage had the gingerbread trim used on larger homes and a wrap-around porch with bracketed turned posts. This home is atypical of Miller homes in being smaller and mostly on a single level. The original paint sported dark trim and porch railings.

The first owner, John Thompson Riner (1831-1915) married Mary Pyne (1835-1894) in 1856 and later Ann Keatley. Dorse "Ebb" (1891-1965) and Maude Lowe (1890-1960) lived there later and then Kit Ballengee (1895-1986).

The home is no longer standing. (Note: John Riner's brother, William C. Riner, also had a home built by Miller.)

*Charming Riner cottage on Kibble Hill, date unknown.
Photo provided by Monnie Martin.*

*John Thompson Riner, date unknown.
Photo provided by Monnie Martin.*

20. GEORGE W. UNDERWOOD: This Victorian home, located near the top of Kibble Hill on Pine Grove Road at Dry Pond, had a spacious front porch with railings supported by turned spindles and decorative scrollwork topping the porch posts. The front facing gable also featured ornate scrollwork in its peak.

The home was likely built in 1899 for George Washington Underwood (1865-1949) who owned and ran his own farm. He married Eliza S. Miller (1871-1941) in 1888 and they had three children, Lillie, Arthur and Charlie. His great-grandson, Pat Broyles, ran the Ballard Food Center. The house has had major renovations in recent years, the removal of the second story, and, later, the rebuilding of the second floor and reshaping of the entire structure so that it bears no resemblance to the original home.

George Underwood home on Kibble Hill.
Photo provided by Mary Burks.

New construction on the first floor of the George Underwood home, 2020.
Photo by Becky Crabtree.

22. ORCHARD STORE: This two-story building stood across the one-lane road from 3389 Pine Grove Road. The front featured a wide upstairs porch supported by tapering square columns, set on brick bases in later years. Large storefront windows gave customers a good view of the general store merchandise inside. The second floor served as living quarters. The store was run by Charley and Dolly Ellison from the 1940s to the 1950s when they moved to Ellison's Store in nearby Ballard. This building served as a residence until it was torn down in the late 1980s.

General Store on Pine Grove Road at Orchard, 1988.
Photo provided by Irene Greene.

23. ANDREW P. MILLER: This Shingle style home is located on Pine Grove Road and has an unusual gambrel roof, a wide wrap-around porch, a half-circle window, and dormers facing east and west. Originally, the porch sported a frieze of tapered pendants painted white so they stood out from the dark trim of the house. The interior walls are covered with narrow inlaid chestnut boards and the wooden fireplace mantel and door and window facings are adorned with decorative concentric circles. The stair railings are supported by turned spindles and the newel posts are topped with rounded, knobbed spheres.

The home was built in 1905 for Adison Plunkett "Plunk" Miller who was a brother of John Campbell Miller's wife, Lillie. The last residents of the home were Samuel "Gene" Humphreys (1918-2004) and Lilly Wesley Humphreys (1923-2018), Fred and Florence Wesley's daughter. There are several pieces of furniture made by Florence and her father, John Campbell Miller, handed down through the family. Clark and Linda Humphreys are the current owners. Clark is the great-grandson of John Campbell Miller.

[Left] Plunk Miller House, about 1910.
[Right] Plunk Miller House, late 1920s.
Photos provided by Clark Humphreys.

CHAPTER FOUR 83

Plunk Miller House, 1970. Photo provided by Irene Greene.

*Aerial view of Plunk Miller place, about 1970.
Photo provided by Clark Humphreys.*

Plunk Miller house, 2019. Photo by Becky Crabtree.

Rolltop desk made from tiger oak by Miller. The rolltop itself is attached to oil cloth giving it flexibility. When the top is pulled down a wooden system of levers fasten the drawers in place, locking them. When it is raised, the drawers can be opened. 2020. Photo by Becky Crabtree.

CHAPTER FOUR 85

*Newell post and stairs in Plunk Miller house, 2019.
Photo by Becky Crabtree.*

*Mirrored dresser made by John Campbell Miller as a wedding gift for his wife Lillie
Belle in 1890, owned by Linda Humphreys, 2020.
Photo by Becky Crabtree.*

Round table made by Florence Wesley, John Campbell Miller's daughter. She worked in the shop with her father and learned woodworking skills. 2020. Photo by Becky Crabtree.

Wooden side tables made by Florence Wesley, John Campbell Miller's daughter. 2020. Photo by Becky Crabtree.

24. **LEONIDAS LIVELY**: Located on Pine Grove Road near Lindside, this Queen Anne style home was originally three rooms, two downstairs, a kitchen and parlor, and one room, a bedroom, upstairs. It is atypical of Miller's houses in being a small cross-gable building, but with a signature cutaway bay window in the front of the building. The one-story addition was not part of the original building.

A stone dairy was built behind the home for food storage. In warm weather, the family often ate in the dairy because the woodburning stove used for cooking made the kitchen uncomfortably warm. A wide wrap-around porch, now enclosed, once graced the front and sides of the home. Trim boards with cutout designs edge the top corners of the front upstairs windows and a half-circle window is centered in the front gable. The two original chimneys remain and one has been restored for use. The date of construction in local tax records is listed as 1920, but a much earlier date, closer to 1905, seems realistic.

The home was built for a farmer, Leonidas "Lon" Marion Lively (1858-1921), and wife Lillie Pleasant Hoke (1865-1943). They married in 1885 and had 11 children: Nannie Lula Blankenship (1886-1930), George William (1887-1949), Leona Peck (1888-1985), Mary J. Carter (1890-1967), Minnie Clark Smith (1893-1951), Cornelius Wilson (1895-1896), Opie Dorsey (1898-1967), Eunice Lois Ryan (1900-1963), Charles Spurgeon (1903-1974), Omar Talmage (1906-1952), and Graydon Corlelia (1909-1974). Additions were made during the time the Lively family lived there. Charles Spurgeon and Graydon Lively were deeded the property in 1933 and sold it to John and Pearl Huddleston in 1939. Pearl enclosed the front porch, by all accounts, because of the wind.

Lon Lively's great-grandfather, Cottrell Lively (1763-1838), came to the area about 1786, having served in the Continental Army as a private dragoon in Colonel Armand's Regiment of Cavalry in Virginia and Pennsylvania and received 200 acres for his service. He acquired additional properties and was able to bequeath hundreds of acres to each of his children.

A local legend, handed down over the years, is that one of the Lively men was called to war. The night before he left, he buried the family fortune, a sack of gold, somewhere on the farm. According to the story, he died in the night. The sack of gold has been the object of searches since that time. At one time, the Lively family farm consisted of more than 1,000 acres which added to the difficulty in finding the unknown location of the legendary buried gold. In recent years, students and faculty from nearby Virginia Polytechnic Institute and State University helped in the search with metal detectors, but without success.

A likely candidate for the main character role of the story is Cottrell Lively's son, Wilson, (1815-1865), Lon's grandfather. He was a captain in Company C, Virginia 166th Militia Infantry Regiment, and was called to return to Richmond in early April 1865. Reportedly, he heard along the way, in Farmville, Prince George County, Virginia, that General Robert E. Lee's surrender was imminent. Lively died immediately of a heart attack, thus never returning home. Wilson had also been a farmer, a landowner of hundreds of acres, the sheriff of Monroe County, and was a member of the Virginia Assembly from 1861-65.

Pearl Huddleston bought the property after Lon Lively's death. The current owner, Mrs. James "Pat" Powell, has lived in the house since 1973 and told the "Legend of the Lively Gold."

*Lon Lively house showing enclosed front porch, 2020.
Photo by Becky Crabtree.*

*Front view of Lon Lively house, 2019.
Photo by Becky Crabtree.*

CHAPTER FOUR 89

*Side View of Lon Lively house showing original, working chimney, 2020.
Photo by Becky Crabtree.*

*The old stone dairy located just behind the Lon Lively house, 2020.
Photo by Becky Crabtree.*

5

The Seneca Trail from Lindside to Fountain Springs

This is a long straight valley along the margin of the area known to geologists as the Allegheny Foldbelt. The linearity was created by gigantic tectonic folds and faults formed in deep geological time and have eroded so that a limestone rock outcrop is exposed. This rock type dissolves easily and over time formed the valley. The valley lacks a stream along much of the length because limestone is prone to underground drainage. This area was not farmed until after the introduction of well-drilling machinery in the early to mid-1800s. Instead, the early farms developed along the almost parallel Rich Creek Valley, upstream and downstream of Woods Fort.

By the 1920s, the federal government established the Seneca Trail, now U.S. Route 219 for automobile traffic and, since then, urban sprawl has crept up to Lindside from Peterstown. Still, breathtaking scenery along this route includes the 3,500-foot mountain ridge, Peters Mountain, which extends for 35 miles along the eastern part of Monroe County.

Miller's work involved a home in Lindside (No. 29) and a number of large farmhouses (Nos. 25, 30-34, and 59) three of which are on side roads, No. 25 on Broyles Cemetery Road, No. 30 off Wilson Mill Road, and No. 59 on Painter Run Road. Note that the houses on U. S. Route 219 were built before the road was straightened, so they may appear somewhat off the road, and may be surrounded by more recent homes, but they started out as farmhouses.

25. JOHN A. BROYLES: This picturesque Queen Anne style home sits at the base of a rolling hill just below the original owner's family graveyard, Broyles Cemetery. The complicated roof line features gables with sunburst ornamentation, semi-circular windows, bracketed window decorations, and a curved front porch.

Tax records indicate the house was built in 1899, but family members say it was built closer to 1905. The first owners, John Alexander Broyles (1862-1917) and Mahala Etta McDaniel (1867-1955) were married in 1888 and they farmed more than 400 acres surrounding the home. They had two daughters, Rosa Lee Spangler (1887-1947) and Pearl Mae Dillion (1891-1986). The farm was divided between the two sisters when their father died in 1917. Rosa Lee and Leonard Spangler's inheritance of 276 acres included the home with the provision "that my wife Mahala Etta be allowed to make her home with them and to have her support from them during her natural life." Pearl and Hugh C. Dillion resided in another home on the farm and they inherited 131 acres with that house.

The road on which the home is located was once called Leonard Spangler Road, but has since been renamed Broyles Cemetery Road, which intersects U. S. Route 219 to the east. There was an attic fire in the 1980s, but the house was saved.

Other owners include Avery Miller, Harry Allen, Melvin and Vivian Harvey, and Dr. John Boone. It is now owned by the estate of J. B. Buckland. Sam and Christy Reece and family live there.

John A. Broyles House, 2018. Photo by Becky Crabtree.

29. MABEL M. BALLARD: This is a lovely example of Craftsman cottage architecture. The emphasis is on crisp horizontal lines with overextended eaves, exposed brackets, and a low-pitched gable roof. The front dormer has a triple window as does the front first floor of the house and there are several double windows elsewhere. The wide wraparound porch is supported by thick, tapered columns. Tan and brown colors on the exterior are traditionally used earthy tones found in Craftsman cottages. The interior features the same clean lines: thick trim around the doors and windows and sturdy newel posts on the stairs. The house, located in central Lindside on Seneca Trail South, U. S. Route 219, may have been built for Dr. Thomas Campbell Green (1877-1965) in about 1925. Green was the first state veterinarian in West Virginia and he served in that capacity for 22 years. The Ballards bought the home from John Odie Coulter (1881-1969) in about 1928. Coulter and his brother, Kenny Ray, grew up in another Miller house, No. 34. Clarence Eugene Ballard (1888-1939), a retail merchant, partner in the Mann-Ballard & Company Store, married Mabel May "Madge" Broyles Ballard (1896-1975), in 1916. They had 10 children who lived in this home: Catherine Julia Dunn (1916-2013), Anna Mae Spangler (1918- 2006), Clarence A. (1920-1970), Thomas Calvin (1924-1964), Garnet Clay (1926-1930), Herbert Clark (1929-1960), Glenn Chambers (1931-1993), James Claude (1933-1956), Benny Curtis (1935-2012), and Sara Jane "Susie" Wickline (1938-2021). Madge ran the store, which had become the Ballard Store, for a short time after her husband's death and then was the first female elected to a Monroe County office. She was the clerk of the Monroe County Circuit Court from 1945-1962.

Alma Louise "Lou" Ballard is the current owner of the home and has resided there for 54 years. She says that her husband, the late Curt Ballard, was born and died in the same bedroom in the home.

"Madge" Ballard House, 1988. Photo provided by Irene Greene.

*Side view, "Madge" Ballard House, 2018.
Photo by Becky Crabtree.*

*Front view, "Madge" Ballard House, 2018.
Photo by Becky Crabtree.*

30. JOHN A. McDANIEL: Nestled at the base of Peters Mountain off Wilson Mill Road, this home is an "L-shaped" traditional two-story farmhouse in the Folk Victorian style. Building materials included beams long enough to run from ground to roof. The original construction included double porches with turned spindles and railings that ran the length of the front. The porches were replaced with a concrete pad and four

columns in 1985. The interior doors have adjustable transom windows directly above them. All the original interior walls were sheathed with tongue-and-groove chestnut boards. Today, that wall treatment remains only in the foyer and stairway and in wainscoting with chair rail molding in the dining room. The central stairs have two landings along with the original railings and urn shaped tops on newel posts. The house has three chimneys and once had a half dozen lightning rods. Local tax records list the home in 1920, but neighbors think it was more likely 1910. A log house was located within a few yards of this site in 1870.

The house was built for the son of John A. McDaniel (1838-1918) and wife, Mary Ann Humphreys (1833-1916), Andrew Pate McDaniel (1868-1956). She was a first cousin of John Campbell Miller's father Wilson Mann Miller (1844-1898). They shared grandparents Henry Miller Sr. (1774-1862) and Rhoda Brooking (1778-1854). Andrew Pate married Sarah Belle McGhee (1880-1945) in 1897. They raised 10 children in the home: Andrew Cecil (1897-1957), Everett Lee (1898-1969), Annie Evelyn Canterbury (1902-2001), Marjorie Brown Coalter (1903-1967), Kathern "Kate" Pence (1906-1994), Sherman Pate (1909-1980), Ruth H. Maddy (1913-1992), Opie Eldridge (1916-1991), Alva Irene Holsambak (1919-2005), and Marshall (1924-2005). There were three large bedrooms upstairs, one for Pate and Sarah, one for the five girls, and one for the five boys.

McDaniel family historian, Cathy McDaniel Levandowski, wrote in 2019, "When Andrew Pate died in 1956, he left the property to his unmarried children, Sherman, Kate, and Marshall, who all still lived in the home. As each married, they gave their share to the others. Sherman was the last to marry and thus inherited the house and property."

It is said that when Andrew Pate died, his body was laid out in the parlor and during the night the floor gave way and the casket crashed through the floor. He and Sarah are buried in the McDaniel Cemetery adjoining the property along with his parents and grandparents.

The house and 112 acres were sold to the Mercer Anglers Club in 1969. The current residents, Roger and Becky Crabtree, have owned the home since 1981.

John A. McDaniel house, about 1916. Sherman McDaniel (born 1908) and Ruth McDaniel Maddy (born 1913). Photo provided by Cathy McDaniel Levandowski.

*Front view, John A. McDaniel house, about 1940.
Photo provided by Cathy McDaniel Levandowski.*

*Side view, John A. McDaniel house, about 1940.
Photo provided by Cathy McDaniel Levandowski.*

CHAPTER FIVE 97

*John A. McDaniel house, 1965.
Photo provided by Cathy McDaniel Levandowski.*

*Front view, John. A. McDaniel house, 2020.
Photo by Becky Crabtree.*

*Interior features of the McDaniel House: stairway and foyer, 2020.
Photo by Becky Crabtree.*

CHAPTER FIVE 99

John A. and Mary Ann Humphreys McDaniel, charcoal drawing, late 1800s.
Artist unknown. Drawing provided by Cathy McDaniel Levandowski.

[Left] John A. and Mary Ann Humphreys McDaniel, about 1900.
Photo on Find-A-Grave, posted by Karyn Schwanen.
[Right] Andrew Pate and Sarah Belle McGhee McDaniel, about 1940.
Photo provided by Cathy McDaniel Levandowski,
obtained from Bonnie Bradley McDaniel.

31. KATHERYN V. DILLON: This stately home sits on a hill north of U. S. Route 219 just south of Lindside. Built on stone pillar foundations, the Queen Anne style house features multiple chimneys and bracketed gables with a bay window on both the northern and southern sides. The wide front porch has spindles supporting the railings. In the back, a stairway and entrance lead to a small room that adjoins the master bedroom on the second floor. This may have been a living space for a servant.

The house was likely built between 1910 and 1917 for Alexander Evans (1830-1917) and his second wife, Roena J. Epperly (1882-1917, m. 1903), who are buried in the nearby Evans Cemetery. Alexander's son Samuel F. Evans (1876-1943) and wife, Catherine "Kate" Raines (1884-1961) lived there after 1917. They married in 1909 and had two sons, Alfred Leroy (1914-1995) and Paul A. (1910-1958).

Others who owned the property over the years were Irene Lawhorn, and Mary E. Ellison. Ellison rented the house at one time to Katheryn Virginia Miller Dillon "Aunt Catheryn," John Campbell Miller's daughter, and her husband, George W. Dillion.

The current owners, Aaron and Alana Terry, were married on the grounds in 2015. They have renovated the home and reside there at this time.

It is not clear why it is referred to as the "Broyles House." Some speculate that a Broyles family may have rented it.

Front view, Katheryn Dillon house, 2018. Photo by Becky Crabtree.

Side view, Katheryn Dillon house, 2018. Photo by Becky Crabtree.

32. WILLIAM H. HANSBARGER: Located on U. S. Route 219 north of Peterstown directly across from Fountain Springs Golf Course, this three-story late Queen Anne style structure features the characteristic curved, wrap-around porch, with classical columns, ornate gables, and a Palladian window as well as several arched windows The lines of the house have changed in recent years because of the construction of a balcony and expansion of living space, but guests can still tie their horses to iron rings in the stone wall at the front. The year of construction is not clear but is likely to have been early 1890s.

The original owner, William Henry Hansbarger (1865-1938), born to John Hill Hansbarger (1815-1874) and second wife Susan Neel (1833-1902), a half-brother of Echols Hansbarger. He married Lilly Mandan Lively (1866-1892).

After her death, he married Anna Salomi Peery (1874-1944) from Burkes Garden, Virginia. They had a son, Thomas Frederick, in 1888, and a daughter, Madge, in 1900. Madge was a nurse in Baltimore at Johns Hopkins Hospital in 1931.

Hansbarger was a farmer and also served on the Monroe County Commission for the term ending in 1920 and was a director of the Peterstown Bank in 1931. Anna was active in the Presbyterian Church and the United Daughters of the Confederacy.

The building has been divided into apartments in recent years and is now owned by Grover Jones, who lives there.

Will Hansbarger house, 2018. Photo by Becky Crabtree.

Side view, Will Hansbarger house 2018. Photo by Becky Crabtree.

33. JOHN ECHOLS HANSBARGER: The unusual rectangular Queen Anne style home looks very similar from the front and rear views. It is a cross-gabled Victorian with the front-to-back gable being hipped and displaying lovely ornaments front and back. The side gables are longer, but with a slightly lower ridge-line. The left gable is clipped, the right is not. There are multiple bay windows. Perched on a knoll on the north side of Seneca Trail South, U.S. Route 219, several miles north of Peterstown, the home's wide wrap-around porch provides a peaceful view of Little Mountain and the valley farmland at its base.

The home was probably built a bit earlier than the 1920 date indicated by tax records. The original owners were John Echols Hansbarger (1859-1925) and wife Julia Lee Clark Hansbarger (1864-1964). They married in 1884. He was appointed postmaster in Lindside in 1887 and was elected sheriff and served for several years. He became the first president of The First National Bank of Peterstown, serving in that capacity from 1910 to 1925. There were six children: Frank, Gladys, Henry, Clarence, Echols, and Julian.

John Echols' parents were John Hill Hansbarger (1815-1874) and Elisabeth Jane Hodge (1824-1859) who married in 1845. John Hill attained the rank of captain and served in the commissary department of the Confederate army. In the 1920 Census, they owned a farm in Red Sulphur township and he is listed as a stock farmer.

H.H. Hardesty's "Biographical Atlas of Monroe County" describes John Echols: "He is a young man of fine attainments, has traveled a good deal, and is now giving attention to the cultivation of a good farm in Red Sulphur District, on Rich Creek, of which he is the owner."

John Echols Hansbarger, date unknown. Photo from Caperton Museum, Monroe County, West Virginia Historical Society.

This residence and land, known as the Locust Hall Farm Company, was run by Mrs. Hansbarger for many years after her husband's death. She managed a herd of Hereford cattle and hosted numerous social events in the family's home.[17] The farm was sold in 1969 to Katherine D. Mitchell and was then owned by the Hall family. Mrs. George Todd's heirs are the current owners. Today, it is only occupied seasonally.

Front view, Locust Hall, Echols Hansbarger house, 2019. Photo by Becky Crabtree.

Rear view, Locust Hall, Echols Hansbarger house, 2019. Photo by Becky Crabtree.

33. JOHN PORTER PATTON HOUSE OF GAP MILLS: This house is a "look-alike" house to that of John Echols Hansbarger. It was most recently owned by the late Evelyn Hansbarger who bought it with her husband Clark about 1980. She told Dr. Ronald Ripley that the original owners of the two houses, John Echols Hansbarger and John Porter Patton, were friends and that her house was copied from the Fountain Springs House. To test this idea, photos of the houses were compared, including aerial photos (mapwv.gov), and these confirmed that the houses are remarkably similar in detail.

The aerial photos showed the houses to be the same size and the floor plans appear to be identical in the following ways: The front-to-back gables of the houses have a ridge line that is continuous and slightly higher than the right-side gable. The ridge lines of the side gables are not continuous as the right one is lower and displaced toward the back of the house about 4 feet. Also, the right gable is clipped, unlike the other three, and this wing of the houses is somewhat narrower than the other three in both cases.

Front View, John Porter Patton house, 2020. Photo by Fred Ziegler.

The ground-level views are also similar in detail including that the porches are symmetrical with respect to the front of the building except that there is a bulge on the right side where the entrance is located in both cases. The window placement is also the same, including several round and semi-circular windows. There are bay windows on the ground floor located on the right side of the front wing and on the left side of the rear wing, again in both houses.

The two differences in the houses are that the Gap Mills house has dormers on the front of the right and left gables while the Fountain Springs house does not, and that the latter has Victorian trim on the front and back gables while the former does not. Also, the Gap Mills house retains its shutters which gives it a more balanced appearance.

It seems that the two houses must have been made from the same plans. Mrs. Hansbarger had told Ripley that they bought the house from a Patton descendant and that the Hansbarger of Fountain Springs was born just two years later than John Porter Patton, who lived at Gap Mills at the time, so this seems to fit. There is no evidence that John Campbell Miller built the Gap Mills house and, indeed, it is well outside the geographical range in which he seems to have operated.

Rear View, John Porter Patton house, 2020. Photo by Fred Ziegler.

34. COULTER: This large Folk Victorian home was located on U. S. Route 219 on the north side of the intersection of the highway and County Route 219/24, now dubbed Wilson Mill Road. The first-floor porch curved around three sides of the home with railing supported by shapely turned balusters framed by bracketed turned columns connected by a frieze at the top.

Both floors were generously supplied with double-hung nine-pane windows and a narrow bay window was located at each end of the façade. Construction took place prior to 1920.

It was first owned by Charles "Charley" Jacob Hansbarger (1872-1949), brother of William Henry Hansbarger and half-brother of John Echols Hansbarger, and Carrie A. Hale (1875-1957). The three Hansbarger homes are less than three miles apart.

The home was sold in 1920 to John Henry Coulter (1857-1927), a farmer. Coulter and his wife, Emaline Ellison (1861-1940) had seven children ages 1 to 19 years old in 1900, including a son, Kenny Ray. Members of the community long remember the death of the younger Coulter, who was killed in a horrendous truck crash in 1963 when the brakes failed on the coal truck in which he was a passenger. Although he attempted to jump from the truck, his clothes became entangled and he was pinned under it at the bottom of a 25-foot embankment near Glen Lyn. Another story handed down about Coulter was that earlier in life he survived being run over by a tractor in the intersection by his home. His wife, Eva Blair Coulter (1903-1987), taught school.

Harry and Christine Dillow Allen bought the home in 1962. The Allens lived there several years. Their son, Robert, remembers that it was cold and drafty and hard to heat. Allen then razed the frame house and built a brick ranch house on this site in 1968. Another son of the Allen's, Roger, and wife, Judy are current residents.

Coulter house, 1988. Provided by Irene Greene.

59. CLARENCE V. SYMNS: This large Queen Anne style house is located on County Route 219/21, also known as Painter Run Road near Lindside. The simple lines may reflect more practicality than other Miller homes of this style. The wide wraparound porch is supported by round columns with square concrete bases and dormers face in two directions. The windows currently have shutters which may not have been part of the original construction. If there were decorative features originally, they are no longer visible.

The home was likely built for Clarence Vincent Symns (1878-1958) prior to 1910. He married Nancy "Nannie" Bane Adair (1875-1954) in 1903 and they had four children: Samuel Young II, (1905-1980), Evelyn Bane (1907-1940), Clarence Vincent Jr. (1910-1987), and Julia Reed Powers (1915-1995). At the time of construction, the property owned by the Symns family ranged from the top of Peters Mountain to Rich Creek, extending a good distance across U.S. Route 219.

Symns grandfather, John Symns (1784-1867) married Elizabeth "Betsie" Peters (1795-1890), daughter of Peterstown's early settler, Christian Peters, in 1814. They owned considerable acreage in the area.

Symns Sr. was a farmer and stockman as well as an elected official. He was a member of the State Board of Agriculture in 1901, and a member of the West Virginia Legislature during two decades beginning in 1910, serving on several state committees.[18] He served as the Narrows Livestock Auction President in 1934 and on the local draft board during World War II. In 1950, he succeeded E. I. Terry as president of the First National Bank of Peterstown.

The house was purchased in 1976 by Lacy and Jacquetta Toney. Their daughter, Lucy Toney Comer, and her family currently live there.

Clarence Symns house, 2018. Photo by Becky Crabtree.

Side view, Clarence Symns house, 2018. Photo by Becky Crabtree.

Clarence V. Symns, about 1955. Ancestry.com. Photo added May 8, 2011, by S. T. Owens.

6

Peterstown

This is the gateway community to western Monroe County and is within two miles of the town of Rich Creek, Virginia, on the New River. It also lies on the Indian trail to Cumberland Gap, Tennessee, although the New River was a substantial barrier and had to be crossed at the Horse Ford and later by ferry until after 1925 when a bridge was built. The streets of Peterstown were laid out in 1803 and waterpower was harnessed on Rich Creek early on. An excellent source of drinking water is found along Scott Branch and today supplies the entire western third of Monroe County. Early in the 19th century, a resort was established near Peterstown called Gray Sulphur Springs, but it went out of business before the time of John Campbell Miller.[19] The Giles, Fayette, and Kanawha Turnpike was laid out in 1837 and a large stagecoach inn still stands on Mill Street in the western end of town. The Norfolk and Western Railroad and the Virginia Railroad were constructed along the New River in 1883 and 1909, respectively.

Miller erected a large school, an office, a store, a bank, and several houses, (Nos. 35-43) in Peterstown. Several were made of brick. Most of the commercial establishments are gone, but the houses that remain are seen on U. S. Route 219 and Mill Street.

35. PETERSTOWN SCHOOL: This large, brick, Richardsonian Romanesque style building opened for its first classes in 1912. The building featured arched doorways and tall windows with rounded tops. Multiple dormers adorn the upper floor as well as

multiple gables front and back. Side doors had porticos and the main front entrance was part of a three-story brick extension. The center of the roof featured a cupola. Students from first to 12th grades matriculated here from 1912 until the population of Peterstown youngsters outgrew the building. There was no graduation in 1918 because of a flu epidemic. In 1949. a new building was constructed for high school students. The elementary school was replaced in 1963. Later, the building became Pennington's Furniture Store. It was razed and the First National Bank of Peterstown was built on the site, 380 Market Street, in 1988.

Peterstown School, 1912. Photo from "Highlights of the History of Monroe County Schools 1799-1999." Monroe County Bi-Centennial Committee, 1999.

CHAPTER SIX   113

Peterstown School, July 21, 1946.
Sunday Register, Beckley, West Virginia.

"Old Peterstown School" sketch by Leigh W. Boggess, 1992.
Used with permission of the artist.

36. E. I. TERRY: Located at the intersection of Thomas and Market streets in Peterstown, this large home is eye-catching. It has a wide wrap-around porch supported with columns, gables facing in all directions, and double chimneys. Inside, the master bedroom has an adjoining room with a separate set of stairs. There is an attic cistern for gravity fed running water, and the overflow in the bathtub is a scant two inches from the bottom of the tub. The house has wide woodwork throughout and decorative fireplace mantels in several rooms. Built in 1907 for E.I. Terry (1877-1961) and wife Annie C. Johnston (1888-1976), it was not originally bricked. A brother of Terry likely did the brickwork. Terry was a merchant and one of Peterstown's most prominent citizens. He was president of the First National Bank of Peterstown from 1934 to 1950, treasurer of the Peterstown Baptist Church, and Rotary's Man of the Year in 1957. After a 1910 fire, he rebuilt his store with a new two-story general store building in 1915 and rebuilt after a second fire in 1937. The Bluefield Daily Telegraph of October 29, 1931, summed up Terry and his enterprise: "The largest store in all of Monroe County is operated at Peterstown by E.I. Terry who has built up a large business by square dealings and friendly relations with his customers. Mr. Terry, born and raised in Peterstown, has been in business there for upwards of 34 years."

The home is currently owned and occupied by Jim and Jodie Posey.

E. I. Terry house, 2017.
Photo by Pamela Agee Jackson.

37. DR. JOHN O. HUNTER: and 38. DR. HUNTER OFFICE: The house is a spacious Prairie style Four-square structure contemporaneous with the Craftsman Cottage style. The building is very similar to a Sears kit house but is not an exact match. It displays a pair of circular windows on the front of the home. Early photos of the home show dark trim on a light background.

Located at 113 Market Street in Peterstown, this was the home of Dr. John Oscar Hunter (1880-1963). Just across Market Street from the home, a vernacular, functional style building was raised to house Hunter's office. It is rather plain, a large, two-story building with an addition on the rear.

Dr. Maggie Ballard wrote of John Hunter's excellence as a student in 1895 at Back Creek School near Greenville; his average was 99.67 percent. In the 1910 census Hunter lived with his brother Will in Greenville. Together, they practiced medicine in Red Sulphur Springs. In 1912, he started his medical practice in Peterstown, and in the same year, married Myrtle Geneva Fleshman Hunter (1890-1967). He made the news by purchasing a car in 1913. The house and office building were likely built about the same time. By the 1920 census, they lived in this house.

By his records, he delivered more than 2,000 babies in the Peterstown area, many as he traveled the area on horseback.[20] They reared two daughters, Nedra and Mary, in the home. His brother, Dr. Will Hunter, went on to operate a hospital in Princeton, West Virginia.

Several decades later, the home was renovated for commercial use; the first floor housed the law office of Wade H. "Jim" Ballard III, U.S. Attorney for the Southern District of West Virginia. The upstairs apartment was the home of prominent local artist Arthur J. "Pete" Ballard, who in 1963 entertained the daughter of Winston Churchill, Sarah Churchill, there during the Christmas holidays.[21] The home is currently unoccupied and is owned by Ballard Investments LLC. The office building has also been remodeled for commercial use and is owned and occupied by Opportunity Knocks, a gaming establishment.

Dr. John O. Hunter home, about 1920. Photo from Peterstown-Lindside photo file in the Caperton Museum, Monroe County, West Virginia Historical Society.

*Dr. John O. Hunter house, 2018.
Photo by Becky Crabtree.*

*Side view,
Dr. John O. Hunter house, 2018.
Photo by Becky Crabtree.*

*Dr. John O. Hunter's office building, 2018.
Photo by Becky Crabtree.*

*Dr. John Hunter (left) and brother, Dr. Will Hunter in Peterstown, 1930.
Ballard photo file, Caperton Museum, Monroe County,
West Virginia Historical Society.*

40. E.I. TERRY STORE: According to a 1915 article in the Bluefield Daily Telegraph, "E.I. Terry, the up-to-date merchant, has moved into his new store building, which is a large two-story structure and covers an entire block. This is said to be among the largest and most modern businesses in Monroe County. Mr. Terry's store resembles a modern city mercantile establishment and it is a safe guess that he does more business than many of the big city stores." The store was originally built in 1897 and reportedly sold "hardware, groceries, dry goods, wearing apparel, drugs, sundries, furniture, and even coffins. The stock is so complete that it is a rare item that cannot be supplied."[22]

It burned in 1910 and was rebuilt on the same site, then again burned to the ground in 1937. At that time, Terry decided to relocate to a lot just across Market Street.[23] There, a complex of three connected brick store buildings still stand.

Miller remodeled one of the first two frame stores, but whatever work he did was destroyed in the fires that destroyed the building. The existing building is presently owned by the Peterstown Preservation Group, a non-profit organization which is renovating it.

The E. I. Terry Store location in 1937.
Inserts show E. I. Terry on left and his wife, Frances "Fannie" C. Terry,
and her sister-in-law, Frances E. Terry.
100 Year Anniversary Calendar, 2010, First National Bank of Peterstown.

CHAPTER SIX 119

Downtown Peterstown: Terry's Store on right adjacent to the First National Bank of Peterstown, 1964. Photo from Pipeline & Gas Journal, source provided by Nally McKenzie.)

The buildings that formerly housed the E. I. Terry Store, 2016. Photo by Becky Crabtree.

41. BANK AT PETERSTOWN: The First National Bank of Peterstown was established at the corner of Market and Mill streets in Peterstown in 1910. The large brick building was upgraded with a new stucco façade within a few years and the front door location was changed from center front to the left front corner. Likely, Miller took part in this remodeling. After the bank was robbed in 1968, the front door was moved back to center front as a security measure. In 1988, a modern, one-story brick bank was built at the other end of town at 220 Market Street where it stands today.

The First National Bank of Peterstown, 1910.
100 Year Anniversary Calendar, 2010, First National Bank of Peterstown.

CHAPTER SIX 121

The First National Bank of Peterstown, about 1960.
100 Year Anniversary Calendar, 2010, First National Bank of Peterstown.

The First National Bank of Peterstown, 1988.
100 Year Anniversary Calendar, 2010, First National Bank of Peterstown.

42. CLARENCE O. HESLEP: This handsome Late Queen Anne style house was originally painted with light walls and dark trim. The house, located at 37 Mill Street in Peterstown, was built about 1920 according to tax records. It features a floating landing, fireplaces in every room, two bay windows, a wrap-around porch, and a built-in china cabinet. Rich Creek, which marks the border between Virginia and West Virginia, flows at the edge of the backyard.

The original owners, Clarence Oren Heslep (1877-1941) and wife Ora Jeanous Keatley Heslep Nolan (1896-1975) reared four children here. Heslep was previously married to Ora's sister, Alena May Keatley, and they had two children, Lucille and Joseph. Alena died in 1915. Virginia and James were born to Heslep and his second wife, Ora. She became the first worthy matron of the Peterstown Chapter 118 of the Order of the Eastern Star at its founding meeting in 1928.

Heslep operated C.O. Heslep Milling in the 1930s, Peterstown Milling Co., formerly Clark's Mill, along with a feed store located near the bridge marking the boundary between Virginia and West Virginia. He was a member of the Peterstown Town Council in 1922.

Walter and Annie Dent, then their daughter Bethel Dent, owned the house in later years; it is currently owned by Robin A. Mann and is unoccupied.

Clarence O. Heslep house, 2018.
Photo by Becky Crabtree.

*Side view, Clarence O. Heslep house, 2018.
Photo by Becky Crabtree.*

*Heslep house, 1998.
Photo provided with permission by
Alison Simpson from ancestry.com.*

*Jenny and Joe Heslep. Heslep grain mill, about 1928.
Photo provided with permission by Alison Simpson from ancestry.com.*

*Heslep Mill at the entrance to Peterstown beside the bridge. It was located at the end of Mill Street about a block from the Heslep residence, 1931.
Bluefield Daily Telegraph, October 29, 1931.*

CHAPTER SIX   125

*Jenny Heslep with Heslep house in the background, about 1928.
Photo provided with permission by Alison Simpson from ancestry.com.*

*Interior features of the Heslep house:
[L] built in cabinet and [R] newel post for stairs, 2019.
Photo by Becky Crabtree.*

43. CLIFTON M. SPANGLER: This home was built in the Colonial Revival style prior to 1910. The façade is symmetrical and the front door has both side lights and a transom light. There was a large front porch and porches that ran the length of the house on the back both at ground level and on the second floor, connected by stairs. Indoor plumbing was added after original construction. The kitchen sink downstairs and the toilet and tub upstairs were connected in a "frugal use of plumbing," according to a resident many years later. The large upstairs bathroom was a former bedroom, accessible only by going out onto the upstairs porch. A kitchen was added to the rear of the original house.

Nally Wilson McKenzie, who remembered her teenage years living there, said that the windows were so high, she, at 5 feet 4 inches, had to stand in the sill and reach high to put up the curtains. She noted that the window sills were comfortable to walk in as they and the walls were a foot thick. She remembers a central staircase, fireplaces in nearly every room, and was told that the bricks for construction were made locally. Ellen Spangler Johnson, granddaughter of the first owner, remembers a room upstairs for a servant, elegant woodwork, a big dining room and a pantry for canned food under the stairs. The home stood on a hill facing the Orchard Addition near downtown Peterstown on the site of the present Kathlyn Apartments at 11 Race Street.

The original owner is likely to have been Clifton M. Spangler (1862-1946), with wife Annie Clark (1868-1928) and their seven children: Everette Morris, Mary L., Fred, Florence Elizabeth, Pansy C., and Lewis Clark "Bus." Spangler was a farmer and was also the postmaster in Peterstown from at least 1922 until 1930. His memories as a child, according to an early history of Peterstown, included "going with his brothers to see the stagecoach 'come in' from Red Sulphur and hearing the horn blow as it came down the hill north of town."

A later owner of the house was Wade H. "Colonel" Ballard II (1904-1992), who acquired it and used it as a rental property. The house was razed in the late 1980s for the apartment complex.

CHAPTER SIX 127

Cliff Spangler house, 1958.
100 Year Anniversary Calendar, 2010, First National Bank of Peterstown.

Fred Clark and Emily Crotshin Spangler in front of the Cliff Spangler house.
Fred was the son of Cliff and Annie Spangler, 1934.
Photo provided by their daughter, Ellen Spangler Johnson.

7

Cashmere and Ballard

These villages are small and serve a farming community along the plateau country that rises from Peterstown to about 2,100 feet at Ballard. This road, now State Route 12, was a turnpike from early times, and it served the resort community of Red Sulphur Springs to the northwest, as well as provided a link with other resorts and towns in Monroe County.

Ballard began with Clayton Ballard's blacksmith shop in the late 1870s. The blacksmith shop also served as the mail depository where residents could drop off letters and pick up mail while Ballard worked fixing carriages and shoeing horses until a post office was built in 1886.

There were once six one-room schools in the Ballard area and they combined into one prior to 1920. There were and still are several churches in the community. The depth of the church's history and importance can be seen at the Ballard Baptist Church where a concrete stoop and steps called a style stands in the front yard even today. It was used for ladies to get on and off their horses or into or out of carriages. The first car in Ballard was a 1914 Model T owned by Murph Jones, who was available for hire to those needing rides to Rich Creek to the train station, about nine miles away. There was a stave mill for barrel making, a broom factory, a barber shop, a dentist, and a furniture and casket-making business. In 1905, Ballard's first store opened and evolved into the Ballard Food Center, a historic landmark on its own merit.

At the time Miller began work, Cashmere was known as Brush Creek and it lies along the fertile valley of this important stream for farming since colonial times.[24] The large homes belie a farming origin for the area and this activity persists although the communities are within easy access of Virginia and serve as "bedroom communities" for this more populated area. The area is rich, scenic, and the houses are still well spaced out.

Miller's work here was mainly in Queen Anne houses and some of the best surviving examples are to be seen in the Cashmere and Ballard area (Nos. 26-28, and 44-48), but this number does include several stores. This route is classified as a Scenic Byway.

Cashmere, about 1900 from the hilltop on the Peterstown side of the village. House 1 is visible on the left and the school is visible near right center as is the back of House 26. Photo provided by Joey Dunn.

1. CHARLIE M. BIVENS: This is said to be the first house built by Miller perhaps as early as 1886. The vernacular style of this home is simple and functional: An L-shaped structure with a small central pillared porch that frames the front entrance facing the Ballard-Red Sulphur Parkway, State Route 12.

An early owner was Charlie Bivens. Bill and Bea Green Meadows also lived in this small home as did Samuel Roy Brown Sr. (1896-1973) and his wife, Mae Heslep Brown (1900-1996) They married in 1926. It was a one-bedroom home until the Browns added a bathroom, enclosed the porch and added another room. Mae taught piano to many young musicians of the era who lived in southern Monroe County. Her piano, a 1918 model from New York, remains in the front hallway. Their son, Samuel Roy Brown Jr., "Sonny," was born in 1935 during the time they lived here and still lives nearby.

Tom Lester purchased the home and he and son Gary lived there. Gary Lester was murdered in the house in August 2015. The current owner, Tammy Long, inherited it from the Lesters. It is currently unoccupied.

Charlie Bivens House, first house built by John Campbell Miller.
Note: State Route 12 is not visible, date unknown.
Photo provided by Irene Greene.

Charlie Bivens house, front view, 2019. Photo by Becky Crabtree.

Charlie Bivens house, side view, 2019. Photo by Becky Crabtree.

26. ARTHUR D. DUNN: Located on Woodson Road in Cashmere, this expansive Victorian style home has been remodeled, but traces of the original design remain. The wraparound porch is as welcoming as ever, but the clean lines of the modern vinyl siding obscure the slender "waistlines" of the gables and any decorative scrollwork is gone. Still, the house's condition belies its 120-year-old age as it was built prior to 1900. It stands as a sturdy testament to the work of the past.

Dr. Arthur Dean Dunn (1863-1933) may have been the first owner. He was wed to Daisy Florence Dunn in 1901 and they had two children, Ruth E. Fletcher and Arthur Dean Jr. He was a "delivery" doctor and rode a horse to make house calls to deliver babies. His office was a small one-story building in the side yard. He is credited with saving the love letters from Confederate soldiers to his Aunt Nancy Louisa Dunn (1838-1913) and also providing her a home with his family in Cashmere during her final years.[25] His obituary reads: "Dr. Dunn was one of Monroe County's most esteemed citizens. He was active in the practice of his profession until the time of his death." It should be noted that among his pallbearers were E.H. Dunn (No. 2), and Dr. John Hunter (No. 37).

The Rev. James Howard Spencer Sr. (1914 -1996) and his wife Lorraine Ingram (1919-2010) bought the house in the late 1950s. Spencer's 43-year ministry in the Ballard Baptist Church influenced many people and he established Ballard Christian School in 1977. The house remains in the Spencer family, recently the property of Timothy Spencer and now owned by his brother, Daniel Spencer, who lives in the home.

Arthur Dunn house, 2019. Photo by Becky Crabtree.

27. ELI HAROLD DUNN: Built prior to 1900, this Victorian home is located on the east side of State Route 12, the Ballard-Red Sulphur Parkway. The two-story home featured a large curved front porch, a bay window, and a steep hipped roof with gables facing west, north, and south.

It was likely built for Eli Harold Dunn (1876-1946), a merchant and farmer in Cashmere. He married Eva Cordelia McClelland (1882-1933) in 1901 and was appointed as Cashmere postmaster in 1914 and also ran a general store there just across the driveway. They had three children, Zula McClelland (1903-1972), a teacher in Monroe County for 37 years, Frances L. Dunn Caine (1906-1970), and Joseph Harold Dunn (1908-1968). The house has deteriorated and is no longer occupied.

Eli Harold Dunn house, 2018. Photo by Becky Crabtree.

28. MARSHALL B. DUNN: This striking Queen Anne home sits beside the Ballard-Red Sulphur Parkway, State Route 12, between Peterstown and Cashmere. It has all the Victorian frills including ornaments crowning the shingle-covered gables, bracket-supported cutaway bays, and fancy turned columns on a porch that wraps around the front and sides of the building. Now painted white, it originally was an intermediate tone with white trim.

Marshall Burlington Dunn (1861-1935) married Lelia Gertrude Dunn (1873-1958) in 1897. According to Vernon and Kathryn Dunn in their family genealogy, "The time had come for a new house. A site was selected on the farm about two miles from Peterstown on the road to Cashmere. It is a beautiful, large house with a broad porch surrounding it. The family moved into it on 17 Jan 1900, and the house has been occupied by the family continuously since that date."

The family's rich tradition varies a bit from the written version. It includes the story that the family moved into the new house on the first day of the new century. The Dunns also wrote, "Lelia was reared on the farm selected by her great-grandparents, John and Mary (Peters) Dunn, and this was the same farm which her grandfather, James C. Dunn, purchased from James Martin and Lewis Allen Dunn. Marshall was a very successful farmer, adding other farms to those owned by his father. He and Lelia reared their family and lived out their lives on the Peterstown-Cashmere Road." The couple who wrote the Dunn family history shared the Dunn surname but were not closely related.

Marshall B. Dunn family moves into their new home, January, 1900.
Photo provided by Marshall Lee Dunn.

136 JOHN CAMPBELL MILLER

There were nine children, Miriam Katherine (1897-1981), Euna Lee (1898-?), Harry Hobart (1900-1964), Mabel Carrington (1902-1976), Nellie Blaine (1904-?), Anna Clay (1906-1982), Quentin Telford (1908-1877), Gladys Campbell (1911-1954), and Emmett Delford 1913-1981). Considering the vintage photograph supplied by the family and estimating that the four oldest children shown in the picture would have ranged in age from 9 to 4, then the picture must have been taken about 1906.

A grandson, Marshall Lee Dunn, son of Emmett Delford, youngest son of Marshall B. and Lelia Dunn currently owns the house. He and his wife, Mary Frances South, married in 1981 and currently live in the home which they have renovated.

Marshall B. Dunn house, 1988.
Photo provided by Irene Greene.

*Christmas time at the Marshall B. Dunn house, 2018.
Photo provided by Mary South Dunn.*

*Marshall B. Dunn house, 2019.
Photo by Becky Crabtree.*

44. CHARLES ALBERT HINES: This two-story Queen Anne style home was located in the community of Cashmere on the east side of the Ballard-Red Sulphur Parkway. It had a rounded wrap-around porch with bracketed posts and balusters. Within the porch was an elegant front bay window. There was scrollwork in the gables and half-circle windows underneath. Double-trim boards enclosed upstairs windows under the edge of the gables.

This home was built for "Uncle" Dick Hines, known officially as Charles Albert Hines (1862-1954), and his wife, Annie Luther Hale (1872-1904) who married in 1896. They had four sons: Dennis Hale (1897-1937), Luther Julian (1899-1983), Charles Oscar (1901-1971), and Anise Alderson (1904-1983). Hines was a farmer who regularly held Monroe County Stockmen meetings at his farm for extension agent presentations. The home is visible in a photograph of the Cashmere community circa 1900, so it was likely built in the late 1890s.

The last resident of the home was Clara Spangler Belcher Hines (1909-1999), widow of Dennis Mason Belcher (1908-1949) and Charles Oscar Hines (1901-1971), president of the Monroe County Court. She taught at Peterstown High School, was principal of Dry Pond School, a 4-H leader, a member of the Daughters of the American Revolution, and raised champion Cocker Spaniels.

The house was razed by its last owner, J. B. Buckland.

Family Reunion at Charles Albert Hines house, 1960.
Photo provided by Jarrod Hines.

*Family Reunion at Charles Albert Hines house, 1960.
Photo provided by Jarrod Hines.*

Charles Albert Hines house, 1988. Photo provided by Irene Greene.

45. FRANK C. BIVENS: This Queen Anne style home sits on a hilltop in the center of the community of Ballard on State Route 12. It has a steeply pitched roof with gables on all four sides. The big wrap-around porch is rounded from the front entrance to the southern side of the home and there are patterned shingles in the gables. Even though the house is now boarded up, it is easy to imagine the 10 children who played there and the little girls who grew up, retired, returned, and sat on that front porch together in their rockers.

According to modern tax records, the house was built in 1915. The first owners were Frank Commodore Bivens (1875-1923) and his wife Clara Josephine Ballard (1876-1921) who were wed in 1899. Frank was appointed as Ballard postmaster in 1913 and was a farmer and a merchant. In addition to the sprawling home, Miller built a small, simple store building that contained the Ballard Post Office just north of the house. It was a grocery store and post office until the late 1950s. After standing empty for many years, the building was hit by a vehicle and was torn down in 2019.

Frank C. Bivens house front, 2019. Photo by Becky Crabtree.

The large family of Bivens children: Everette Duane (1900-1975), Vivian Rose (1902-1997), Nina Ellen Keffer (1904-1989), William Oren "Dink" (1908-1985), Gladys S. (1905-1975), Anna Clayton Ferrell (1906-2001), Louise D. Webb (1910-1982), Elaine Ruth (1915-1987), Frank Commodore Jr. (1918-1993) and Howard Hunter (1920-1974) lived in the house. When "Dink" and his brother Howard went off to World War II, their wives, Hyla Johnson (1913-1954) and Evelyn Jeanette Ward (1925-2005), respectively, remained there with the family. Louise and Gladys maintained the home into their later years and Howard came back to live there later in life. He was the last resident of the home. It was owned by Dink, who built a smaller home behind it for Hyla. After her death and his subsequent marriage to Callie Rosetta in 1956, they remained in the smaller home.

Dink was a school principal and across the road he built Ballard's Dairy Bar which he managed during the summer months. The home is no longer occupied and was inherited by Dink's stepson, George W. Bostic.

Frank C. Bivens house side porch, 2019. Photo by Becky Crabtree.

*Frank C. Bivens house in Ballard, 1988.
Photo provided by Clark Humphreys.*

47. BALLARD FOOD CENTER: The Ballard Food Center has a long, rich history. It opened for business in 1905 and was a country store and community gathering place until 2012. Located across the Ballard-Red Sulphur Parkway at the intersection of Orchard Road, fresh produce, plants, locally made jellies, jams, and groceries were part of the varied stock. Although the exact date of the residential addition is not known, it was pictured in a sketch when the parkway was unpaved, making it likely that it was added soon after the 1905 store opening. The two-story wing housed a three-bedroom apartment. The second floor of the store housed another apartment until converted to a storage area. There were both indoor and outdoor stairs and a double-decker porch with the bracketed porch posts used often in Miller's construction.

An early owner was Doc Witt but it is unclear if he was the original owner in 1905 or if it was W.O. Woodson. Woodson offered a set of dishes, one piece at a time depending on how much the customer spent on groceries. There was a bowl in a display case in the store decades later as a reminder of the incentives of the past. He had a large warehouse in Rich Creek, Virginia, and another one across the road in the old Ballard Post Office. Woodson went on to be the president and general manager of Virginia

Grocery in Narrows, Virginia. Years later, his only child, Sue, became a chemist and worked on the Manhattan Project during World War II.

In the 1920s, a Mr. Reed took over. Then, Eva Hodge ran the store followed by Harvey Mann in the 1940s. Mann had a barbershop and a post office along with the store known then as the Harvey Mann General Store.

Lonnie and Elizator Lane were the proprietors for several years in the 1950s. Hans Creek resident Paula Oliver Mann recalls those years: "I remember there was an old coal stove in the middle of the store toward the back and men would be sitting around it talking. If the store was not too busy Lonnie would be back there talking to them. They had a bench out on the store porch where the local young people would sit and talk and greet those coming into the store. Everyone knew one another back then."

Donnie and Patty Jones ran it for a while after that. Lonnie and Elizator returned, but illness made them unable to manage the store. Their daughter Nora Lee and her husband Pat Broyles bought the store in June 1973. The store and the Broyles couple had found a good match in one another for the next nearly 40 years. They sold a lot of groceries and produce and gave away much good will until their retirement in 2009 when the store was sold to Richard McBride. It burned beyond repair in 2012.

Ballard Food Center, residential addition on the right, about 1995. Photo by Oliver Photography, used with permission, provided by Nora Lee Broyles.

Painting of Ballard Food Center, drawn by Jill Skidmore in 1987 using a photo from the early 1900s. Sketch provided by Nora Lee Broyles.

48. SAMUEL O. BROYLES: Built in 1912, this two-story Queen Anne style home may have been changed from its original design, possibly with more modern siding and removal of decorative appendages, but it maintains a generous wraparound porch, gables facing in three directions creating a complicated roof line.

It is located on Adair Ridge Road near Ballard. There is speculation that it may have been built by another builder, Alex Humphreys, which would also account for the differences in style. The first owner was probably Samuel Overton Broyles (1882-1960) who first married Maud Smith (1884-1906) in 1904 and Minnie B. Crotty (1883-1971) in 1908. There was a daughter with Maud, Stella Mae Broyles Riley (1905-1991), and three sons with Minnie, Stanley Crotty (1915-1968), Theodore Roosevelt "Teddy" (1919-1991), and Garnet Julian (1922-1986).

Broyles was also known as "Obie" and "Ovey." He was a farmer and sold alfalfa in the 1930s for 80 cents a bale. A long-time resident of Ballard, Norman Thompson, says Broyles had a sawmill and remembers riding a horse to the farm to pick cherries. Apparently Broyles was also an entrepreneur as he sold lots in the "S.O. Broyles Addition" in Ballard, and, with his brother, George Finley "Finn" Broyles (1893-1977), purchased a furniture and casket-making business. They first moved it to the field across from the present Ballard Baptist Church, later moving it permanently to a shop at the foot of Ballard Mountain on State Route 12. The shop was in a two-story block structure still in use. He could reach the business by hiking or riding horseback through the woods from his residence. He was a carpenter, built his own casket, and was pictured with it prior to using it. The house was remodeled by Garnet Julian "Bus" Broyles and was subsequently owned by Franklin Dale Broyles. It is currently owned by Billy and Melva Wheeler.

Samuel Overton Broyles house, 2020.
Photo by Becky Crabtree.

*Samuel Overton Broyles house, side view, 2020.
Photo by Becky Crabtree.*

*S. O. Broyles with coffin he built for himself, prior to 1960.
Photo provided by
Pamela Agee Jackson.*

Unlisted: BURNICE FARLEY: This home is tucked in a narrow valley between rolling hills near Bunker Hill. Its long driveway from Pine Grove/Bunker Hill Road crosses a creek and a long flat pasture. The six-room home has an angular porch on two sides and gables facing in three directions. Various outbuildings and barns dot the edges of the yard.

It was built in 1905, according to tax records. At that time the land was owned by Alexander F. Matthews, a lieutenant in World War I who died of his wounds. Just prior to the war, he sold to William Adair Fleshman (1882-1941) and wife, Ida Dillon. Afterward, Burnice Dee Farley (1915-1998) and brother Charles Mark Farley (1921-1977) purchased the property together and the men shared the home. Burnice married Ethel May Shepard (1917-1990) in 1935 and moved near New River. Later, about 1947, they moved to this home with daughter Elizabeth Ann Francis (1937-) when their residence was taken by the building of the Bluestone Dam.

Elizabeth Francis has fond memories of growing up in this beautiful setting. She remembers being told that Paxton Mann helped build the house. Francis is the widow of former First National Bank of Peterstown President Tom Francis and she is the current owner. The house is no longer occupied.

(A photo of this home with the identification handwritten on the back was found in the materials compiled by Florence Wesley and Irene Greene, much like the other photos, but it was not numbered, or on their list. Since the possibility exists that it should be included, this information is provided.)

Burnice Farley house, 2020. Photo by Becky Crabtree.

8

Red Sulphur Springs and Indian Mills

The springs were an anchor point on the old Indian trail up Indian Creek located at Red Sulphur Springs, and they were developed as a resort early in the 19th century.[26] The water is sulphur rich and flows out of a limestone layer near the mouth of Fitz Valley. At one time, there were about 18 structures serving the resort, from hotel and "connecting cabins" to stables and a bandstand.

People visited the area to cure everything from drunkenness to hay fever,[27] to the itch, to sore legs, to skin diseases.[28] Water from the spring was bottled and sold as far away as New York City.[29] Stories are still told about the resort's cooks adding a little castor oil to the bread, not enough to taste, on the guests' first dinner. It helped their digestion and they quickly felt better. Some guests were too sick to be cured at the springs. Maids were told to close the door quietly and leave if they encountered a dead guest. The body would be taken down the back stairs at night and buried in the cemetery on the hilltop nearby. It was not good publicity to do so during the day.[30] The new and popular hit song, "Home, Sweet, Home" was not allowed to be played by the resort's musicians because it made the mothers homesick and obstructed the cure.[31] Red Sulphur specialized in patients with consumption (tuberculosis) although it also attracted tourists and was on the circuit with Salt Sulphur, Blue Sulphur, and Sweet Springs. There were turnpike connections to all these places as well as to the railroad at

Lowell in the Greenbrier River Valley, so this was a bustling place. Martin Van Buren and Francis Scott Key were both said to be guests at the resort. During the Civil War, Red Sulphur served as a hospital for both Northern and Southern soldiers. After this, the resort struggled into the 20th century, so Miller worked in this area at the end of its glory days, and, by the 1920s, the remaining resort buildings were simply torn down.

Miller built a huge store, a beautiful church, and a number of houses (Nos. 49-56). One of the houses is down the valley to Indian Mills about four miles, and another is upstream along Indian Creek. Once a thriving community with stores, several doctors and a dentist, a community building, a livery stable, several churches, a dance hall, a school, and hundreds of visitors, Red Sulphur Springs nowadays is a much quieter place along State Route 12 with scattered farms and residences.

Indian Mills, an even smaller community is found nine miles from Red Sulphur Springs, just across the Summers County line. It lies along the New River and today is primarily a recreation area with state-run camping and hunting areas. In Miller's time, before the building of the Bluestone Dam at Hinton, which took several residences and a fair amount of land, the community was more affluent. Dr. Dorsey Ryan was one of the residents during that era and had Miller build his home and office there (No. 56).

49. RED SULPHUR SPRINGS CHURCH: The vernacular style of this little country church adds to its charm. Bits and pieces of the practical and beautiful come together to make an interesting, cherished building: a small round window above the double door entrance, six stained glass windows, and a belfry. It was built in 1895.

The church is located at 304 Indian Creek Road at Red Sulphur Springs. A booklet detailing church history reads: "John Campbell Miller moved his planing mill to the church site where he made the weatherboarding and outside finish lumber from kiln-dried yellow poplar. The ceiling and inside finish lumber were constructed of yellow pine. Your close inspection of the finish work of the interior of the church shows the trademark of the fine craftsman Mr. Miller was. The pulpit and original pews were also crafted by him." Through the years, many have contributed beautiful items to the church. In the mid 1920s, Judge C.W. Campbell presented the stained-glass windows and a piano. His brother, Dr. Lewis Campbell, had a Delco-Light plant installed in an outbuilding that provided lighting and replaced the oil lamps. The Roxie Spangler Miller family (youngest sister of the Campbell men) presented the electric lamps now used in the chandelier. Kit and Neva Ballengee donated chairs for use at the secretary's desk. Trixie Martin's family presented the baptismal bowl.

The churchyard contains a cemetery and a monument in honor of the Confederate dead. Dr. Lewis Campbell presented the monument placed in the church graveyard. The building and grounds are well-maintained and church services and events are still held there.

CHAPTER EIGHT 151

*Red Sulphur Springs
Church, 2019.
Photo by Becky Crabtree.*

*Chandelier in Red Sulphur
Springs Church, 2019.
Photo by Becky Crabtree.*

An example of stained-glass windows at Red Sulphur Springs Church, 2019. Photo by Becky Crabtree.

Interior, Red Sulphur Springs Church, 2019. Photo by Becky Crabtree.

50. HUMPHREY'S STORE: This large general store was located at Red Sulphur Springs near the intersection of the Ballard-Red Sulphur Parkway and Indian Creek Road. At that time, it was near the turnpike entrance to the Red Sulphur Springs Resort. It stood three-and-a-half stories high with front porches on the first three floors and multiple gables on the front and side of the massive building. The porches were supported with bracketed posts and lined with balusters. The Red Sulphur Springs Post Office was located in this building.

According to Morton's History of Monroe County, the merchant in charge there was Samuel Finley Humphreys (1856-1904). Long-time Ballard resident, Ellen Spangler Johnson, reports her uncle, Robert Crotshin, and cousin, Earl Ellison, also worked there. The photo was taken in 1906. The structure was burned by arsonists in about 1932.

Humphreys Store, date unknown.
Photo from John W. Dumont's "Background Survey of Red Sulphur Springs."

Humphreys Store, 1906. Photo provided by Clark Humphreys.

51. DR. LEWIS M. CAMPBELL: This large three-story home was built by Otis Heslep and Miller. "Everything was built double: double windows, double roofs, double floors, according to Dr Campbell's wishes."[32] Wide porches completely surround the second and third stories, bordered by square posts and scrollwork balusters. It was built in 1923.

Dr. Lewis McClure Campbell (1863-1935), the original owner, practiced medicine as a coal camp doctor in Eskdale, West Virginia, on Cabin Creek for many years. He returned to his birthplace to build an "immense manor house" then married Virginia Dunn (1884-1970) in 1928. He was 64 at the time of his marriage.

Campbell's office was on the second floor and he lived in the upper level. The ground floor was a garage as well as a large storage area. He was a colorful character in Red Sulphur Springs, and as most doctors of the day were, a bit rough in his treatment. One Ballard resident remembers a woman who went to the doctor with a bealed (abscessed) tooth. He lanced it without use of any numbing agent. She told how she came up out of the chair. Campbell referred to him as "Diamond Lew" because he had a diamond tie pin that he often wore. He was very competitive especially with his brother, Judge C. W. Campbell (1856-1935).

One story tells of the judge buying a purebred male hog and arranging for his friend, Mr. Heslep, to keep it and charge a breeder's fee for local farmers to bring their sows and avail them of the service. This was a popular plan, well-liked by the farmers in the community. Doc Campbell had to top it, so he bought another purebred hog, got Bill Helvey to feed it, and let farmers breed their sows without a charge, topping his brother in popularity for the moment.

Another tale is told that Doc wanted the land on which the Red Sulphur Springs Resort stood (after it closed) and he wanted it cheap, so he hired men to burn the buildings. He was caught and his brother, the judge, helped keep him from serving jail time.

Dr. Campbell died after a long illness and was buried in the Campbell Cemetery on the mountain top of the Isaac Campbell farm along with his parents. He asked in advance that no cars go to his grave and asked George Beasley to drive the wagon carrying his casket. He even asked for his favorite horses, "Pipin" and "Maude," to pull it. He had a fence built around his grave site without a gate. When asked why he didn't include a gate, he answered, "Surely I will have enough friends to get my body over the fence."

His will stated that all his possessions were to go to his wife, Virginia, except for a Pierce-Arrow car that he bequeathed to his youngest sister, Roxie Campbell Miller.

His widow inherited a 117-acre estate, all hills, and she gave away 60 acres for the creation of the nearby Ruritan Park. Years later, local lore tells of a bowling alley in the building and a large room for dances on Saturday nights. The house is now owned by Jack and Susan Parker and is rented.

Dr. Lewis M. Campbell home and office, 1980.
Photo provided by Clark Humphreys.

*Dr. Lewis M. Campbell home and office, 1988.
Photo provided by Irene Greene.*

*Dr. Lewis M. Campbell home and office, rear view, porches
completely encircle the building, 2020. Photo by Becky Crabtree.*

52. **CHARLES W. CAMPBELL:** This Queen Anne style house is set in a picturesque valley by Indian Creek with a backdrop of seemingly undisturbed rolling mountains. The large house is castle-like in its intricacies and provides a glimpse of a bygone era. The porch rounds both corners of the front and is adorned with turned spindles both near the porch ceiling and on the porch floor supporting the railings. The porch posts are bracketed. Wide trim boards drape the corner second-floor windows. The siding on the gable is done with patterned shingles in double rows and with plain shingles between, also in double rows, and there are decorative pieces in the peaks of gables on the front and side of the home. It is a grand old house.

Miller is quoted as saying that he built two houses for Dr. Lewis M. Campbell. We know of a later home built 1.7 miles from this one in 1923, but this home was listed on tax records in 1901 with little evidence to suggest that the doctor ever lived here. It is possible his brother, Judge Charles William Campbell (1856-1935) may have lived here for a time. He practiced law in Huntington and was once the mayor there. When he retired, he moved back to an "ancestral home" in 1924, according to his obituary, but, by then, the house belonged to another family. He may well have spent time here. It is well known that he lived at the old Dunn farm in Red Sulphur Springs for about three years before purchasing another estate near Pickaway, West Virginia. It is also possible that the house was built for his parents in the late 1800s. The cemetery in which Dr. Lewis M. Campbell, his wife, and his parents, Robert Dunbar Campbell (1818-1895) and Mary Catherine Johnson Campbell (1830-1904) are buried lies on the mountaintop above the home.

Campbell/Long homeplace, side view, 1988.
Photo provided by Irene Greene.

The farm where the house was built is known locally as the Isaac Campbell Farm. At least some of the property was owned in the late 1880s by Thomas J. Biggs (1825-1893) and wife, Sarah J. (d. 1909). There is a period during which the owner is unknown, but by 1915, the property belonged to Allen Madison Long (1849-1935). It was inherited by his son, Oral Jefferson Long (1885-1956) and his wife Sarah Ardella Lawrence (1883-1962) They married in 1906. It was then owned by Ernest Weldon Long (1914-1990) and his wife Nellie Gray Ballard (1914-1973) who married in 1935. Three generations of large Long families prospered in this home. It is now owned by Ardella "Tootie" Long Campbell, daughter of Ernest and Nellie Long, with her husband Ralph Campbell. The house is not occupied.

*Campbell/Long homeplace across Indian Creek, 2018.
Photo by Becky Crabtree.*

CHAPTER EIGHT 159

Campbell/Long Homeplace, 2019. Photo by Becky Crabtree.

53. CHARLES L. DUNN: This stately farmhouse stands near the crossroads at the center of Red Sulphur Springs on property that was granted to Nicholas Harvey in 1795. The building date is unknown, as is Miller's involvement, which is described as a "remodel." The front is plain and side-gabled with chimneys at either end and divided windows over the central door, very much in the Federal style. From this we assume it was built early, probably by Nicholas Harvey (1726 - death date unknown) or his son James (1788-1861), and both are buried on the farm.

The Dunn family, Charles Lewis Dunn (1854-1915) and his wife Louisa Jane Spangler, came later and Vernon and Kathryn Dunn provided the following information about them. "They owned the livery stables and stage line which operated between the railroads on New River and the resort hotels at the Sulphur Springs of Monroe and Greenbrier counties. His most noted driver was Wade "Shug" Spangler, half-brother to Louisa Jane. Stories were legend about his skill and experiences handling the six-horse teams used to pull the big three-deck coaches. It was said he could 'turn a stagecoach and six horses in the narrow streets of Peterstown without bumping the heels of any horses on a singletree," (the crossbar of the harness). They add that the need for drivers disappeared because of the decline of the resorts around 1900. The Dunns owned the farm at the time Miller was active and it seems likely that he built the wing extending from the center of the back, or a cross wing behind that. Both portions have double-decked porches similar to other Miller buildings.

In more recent times, Bill Redmond sold the property in 1949 to Hallie Dickinson when she was forced out of the New River Valley in 1949 because of the construction of Bluestone Dam. Eventually the farm was transferred to her niece Linda Roles and her husband, Richie, who developed a business in supplying carriages and drivers for weddings and other occasions. It was finally sold again in 2019 to Abner Kinsinger.

Charles L. Dunn house, 2018. Photo by Becky Crabtree.

Charles L. Dunn/Redmond house, 1980. Photo provided by Irene Greene.

CHAPTER EIGHT

54. LEWIS A. FLESHMAN (no photo available) and **55. JANIE SHEPPE FLESHMAN**: Located on Indian Mills Road, this Craftsman Cottage style home features a full-length front porch and a pair of gabled dormers on the front roof. The low-pitched, side-gabled roof is also an obvious hallmark of this style. Original details are hidden by modern renovations, but the house maintains its sturdy coziness and emphasis on horizontal lines.

The house was built for Dr. William Lester Hunter (1872-1946) and his wife Josephine Emma Weikel (1876-1954). They were married in 1896. It is likely that the home was built in about 1900. Hunter practiced medicine in Red Sulphur Springs before moving to Princeton where he operated the hospital from 1931-1945. He was fondly remembered as a banjo player. A separate structure was built in the side yard as a doctor's office, but it is not clear if it was used by Hunter, a general practice physician, or the brother of a later owner, Dr. Robert Sheppe, a dentist, or both. The office was purchased by Dr. Craig Mohler, disassembled and moved to Union.

The home had several owners early on, Guy Dickison and then Lewis Allen "Teets" Fleshman (1856-1938), who previously lived in No. 54, a home built by Miller across the road on the site now occupied by Homer Long's more modern ranch house. This is what Maggie Ballard said about Fleshman's nickname: "When Lewis Allen was a boy a circus came to the community (Peterstown) and pitched the tent near his home. He spent so much time at the show grounds following the manager around that he has ever since been known by the name of 'Teets' from the name of the circus 'Teets' Traveling Circus and Animal Shows.' "

Fleshman's wife, Jenneta "Janie" Armstrong Sheppe Fleshman (1886-1953), lived in the house after her husband's death. She taught in the public schools of Monroe County for 32 years and was a musician and a piano instructor. Her musical composition "Inauguration March" was copyrighted in 1913. Billy Hodges was a more recent owner. The current residents, Julie and Rodney Bragg, have been owners since 1985.

Janie Sheppe Fleshman house, rear of Charles L. Dunn house in the background, 2019. Photo by Becky Crabtree.

Janie Sheppe Fleshman house, front view, 2019. Photo by Becky Crabtree.

"Inauguration March," composed by Janie Armstrong Sheppe Fleshman in 1913. She was a student of Irene Long, local school teacher and pianist for many years. Music from the Caperton Museum, Monroe County, West Virginia Historical Society.

56. DR. DORSEY McNEIL RYAN: This smaller Queen Anne home was built about 1908. It has eye-catching gingerbread ornamentation in the gables and a wrap-around porch with turned posts and decorative brackets. The roof is complex, allowing for cross gables and a main roof with a gable-on-hip at each end. The office is a separate building located near the home with similar scrollwork in the gable's peak in the front. The house is located in Summers County on Indian Mills Road near Forest Hill.

It was probably first owned by Dr. Dorsey McNeelas Ryan (1877-1945). He was born near Red Sulphur Springs, son of William Francis and Elizabeth Mann Ryan. After graduating from Concord College, Ryan taught school for a few years before going to medical school. He began practicing medicine in Talcott and Indian Mills prior to 1906 when he set up a joint office in Hinton with Dr. Robert W. Timberlake, then established his own office two years later and continued his medical practice until the fall of 1944.

He married Thelma Inez Rose Ryan (1906-1980) in 1930. They had a son, Dorsey McNeelas Ryan, Jr. (1931-2008). Ryan was a captain in the U.S. Medical Corps in World War I and was in the reserves in World War II. He was active in the community as a member of the Kiwanis Club, the American Legion, and the Democratic Party. He railed against parking meters in Hinton, calling them "injurious to local business," ignored them, and went to court to try to prove them illegal. His sister, Maude Ryan Lowe, lived in another Miller home on Kibble Hill, No. 19, the old Lowe Home).

The present owner, Rusty Simmons, uses the structure as a seasonal home. He reported that he was told that the house had been moved from the original site, which was closer to Indian Creek across a field behind the current location.

This is the only Summers County house on the list.

Dr. Dorsey McNeil Ryan's house in Indian Mills, 2018. Photo by Becky Crabtree.

*Dr. Dorsey McNeil Ryan's office in Indian Mills, 2018.
Photo by Becky Crabtree.*

*Postcard showing Dr. Ryan's office by the Redmond, Pauley & Co. Store in Indian Mills. It is postmarked 1908.
Provided by the Caperton Museum, Monroe County, West Virginia Historical Society.*

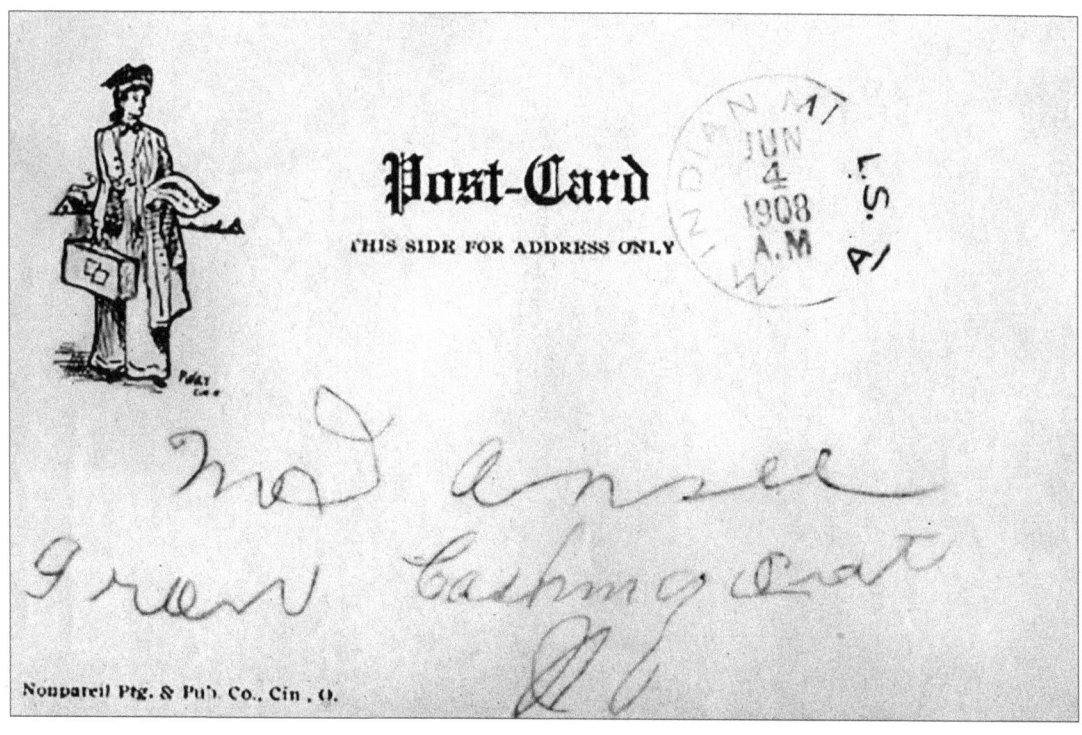

9

McDowell County Homes

The abundance of coal has always played a part in the history of McDowell County, West Virginia, but never more so than in the early 1900s. The population grew 155 percent from 1900-1910. New coal mines were opening and the need for a shipping method was answered by the railroad. The Pocahontas coalfields were booming and the Norfolk & Western Railway played a great part in transforming the county. The boom required new branches of the railroad to be built and many mining companies were springing up, hiring and paying well. Sawmills were thriving and roads were being built. There was a huge need for housing.

Miller responded to the need. He took a crew and built dozens of bungalow style homes for railroad workers in Pageton and Welch and rows of larger, eight-room houses for the foremen and bosses in the mines at Elkhorn. Miller recalled making a profit on providing all of the labor on an eight-room house for $160. According to information provided by his daughter and granddaughter: "Burley Miller (a distant cousin) took Papa's team of horses, named Pete and Frank, with a loaded wagon and drove to these locations and stayed and worked them until the job was finished."

Houses built for the Norfolk and Western Railroad in Pageton, West Virginia over 100 years ago, 2019. Photos by Becky Crabtree.

CHAPTER NINE 169

Houses built for the Norfolk and Western Railroad in Elkhorn, West Virginia over 100 years ago, 2020. Photos by Becky Crabtree.

Houses built for the Norfolk and Western Railroad in Elkhorn, West Virginia over 100 years ago, 2020. Photos by Becky Crabtree.

10

Concluding Observations

West Virginia is a great place for preserving historically interesting buildings. The low population density and low rate of redevelopment results in many small villages with original buildings, including mills, and intervening farmland with picturesque barns and large farmhouses. In Monroe County, the career of John Campbell Miller around the turn of the last century coincided with the arrival of the railroads and a burst in productivity and prosperity. For the first time, farmers could drive their stock to the railheads in a day, so this began a period of farmland expansion. The result was a host of beautiful new homes.

Admittedly, about a third of these buildings have been lost to fire, to changing tastes, or to redevelopment in larger towns (Appendix B). As one farmer put it: "These old houses were drafty, hard to heat, and to maintain properly." Also, it seems that a disproportionate number of the public buildings, like the stores, banks, and schools have succumbed to redevelopment, especially in Peterstown. In the countryside, many of the farms were remote from the fire stations and this was a problem. Nonetheless, there is a legacy of lovely Victorian farmhouses to be proud of.

Today, a majority of the structures are painted white, especially the huge Queen Anne houses. What ever happened to "The Painted Lady," one might well ask? The New Oxford American Dictionary defines the term thusly: "A Victorian house, the exterior of which is painted in three or more colors, effectively highlighting the architecture." For examples, see the collection of 75 plates from the Scientific American ranging in age from 1885-1894 and compiled by Blanche Cirker (1996). These buildings were designed by many architects and span states from the Northeast to the Midwest. The colors range from browns to tans, greens and reds, and they do seem to emphasize the towers and gables and trim as well as differentiating the floors.

The vintage pictures in this book seem to show original paint jobs of about a dozen Miller homes and, of course, only the tones, not the colors, can be seen. The majority were painted light, probably white, with dark trim. The exception is the Marshall Dunn House (No. 28) in which the walls were of intermediate tone and the trim was white. One of the houses (No. 23) does have a dark color to emphasize the triangular shape of the gables and in some cases, the face of the gable was shingled, so stain would have been used. This is the only nod to "The Painted Lady" concept that is observable in our vintage pictures. Miller did engage in a bit of fancy painting when it came to the porch railings. Here the top and bottom rails were dark like the trim on the house, and the supporting columns were dark in the lower and upper part, that is, opposite the point where the two rails intersect and at the top, opposite the light color brackets (see Nos. 11 and 19). The effect was to frame the light colored balusters of the railing and to emphasize the brackets at the top. Dark rings were also used to emphasize the turnings on the columns. Blinds were not generally used on the Queen Anne houses, here or in the big city, but with other styles they were, and seem to have been painted dark. In conclusion, Miller had a traditional streak after all.

Today, three of the Monroe County Queen Anne houses display color on the walls with white trim. Light grey has been used by the Henritzes' (No. 5) and Powell's (No. 24) while tan has been used by the Ashleys' (No. 10). Finally, the Reeces' Queen Anne sports a bright red roof for a totally different look. At least somebody is trying to relieve the monotony.

Appendices Introduction

There are two appendices in this book. The first consists of the original unretouched list of Miller houses available to us, and this appears to have been prepared by his daughter, Florence Miller Wesley, and granddaughter, Irene Wesley Greene.

For most of these houses, an owner's name is provided, often a nickname, and sometimes not the original owner of the house. Nonetheless, this list has been invaluable in preparing this book, together with a picture file prepared by the same women in 1988 for the buildings that were extant at the time. This picture file was obtained from the estate of Irene Wesley Greene with the help of her son, Johnny Greene of Beckley, while the original list was found in the archives of the Monroe County Historical Society. The 1988 pictures have handwritten comments on the back, which are similar, but not necessarily identical, to the comments on the original list, so they must have been available to the photographers in 1988. The comments on the pictures often elaborate on the information available on the list so they have been informative.

The second two-page list is our attempt to update the original one, using the same number system in Column 1, from 1 to 59. Note that one house was not numbered on the original, so we have inserted the number 9A, making the total 60 houses. The "Early Owner Column" gives the full name of an early prominent owner of the building. Why the original owner's name was not used in all cases is unknown to us, although we surmise that the name used was the one familiar to the women at the time the list was made. In some cases, only a surname is given, so we have selected an appropriate family member to insert into our list. We try in the text of this book to explain the complete history of each building insofar as it is known to us, so please search there if there are any questions regarding ownership. "Column 3" gives an abbreviation of the community name, according to the seven chapter headings in the body of the book.

The "Date Column" is incomplete because accurate information is difficult to obtain. Dates are provided for most buildings in the online database, mapwv.gov/parcel, but can be shown to be unreliable. This online site is otherwise invaluable in providing property parcel boundaries, aerial photo images, topographic maps, recent sale information, even early turnpike names, but you need to explore it fully to find all these things.

The "Style Column" contains abbreviations of the building styles used by Miller and these correlate with the list in Table 2. This column also gives a few entries as "remodel," which are for buildings to which Miller made significant additions, but which defy stylistic assignment. In a few cases, you may notice that the original list does use the word remodel while we do not, and in these cases, Miller transformed the house to a significant degree and we have made a stylistic assignment for the portion that he built.

Finally, the current owners are listed for the buildings that still stand, while the fate of the remaining buildings is given in parentheses, about one third of the total. In the text of this book we supply descriptions for most of the buildings on the list except for a couple, Nos. 21 and 46, for which we have not been able to find any significant information. The street addresses are not provided out of consideration for the privacy of the owners. For those who want to find the buildings, let the pictures in this book be your guide, and have fun driving around each neighborhood looking for them, like we did. Please be considerate of the owners.

Appendix A

Houses J. C. Miller built
I copied them down as Mother told me adding the extra "little bits" just like she related them to me.
1. The first house he built was for Charlie Bivens (Dink"s uncle) at Cashmere where Bill and Bea Meadows used to live.
2. The Last house was for Johnny Ryan on Kibble Hill where Emma and Mable lived.

In Greenville
3. Bert Dunlop
4. Ike Ballard
5. Bub Arnett   The Old Parsonage
6. Long Store
7. Frank Maddys house, in back of store
8. Jack Johnsons, across the creek at Greenville
9. Robert Riners   At Wayside. Burned

He remodeled Aunt Mary Jane Pence's home. This is Dewey Pence's Mother. Otis Pence lives there now.

10. Young Home. Where Dalton's lived. This Mrs. Young's daughter was Jack Johnson's first wife. (On the road where Arther Dean and Sylva lived)
11. The Dewey Pence home where Mrs. Coon lived
12. Dunlap Home (Harrett Ellison Dobbs lived)
13. Letch Miller Home.. (has been remodeled)
14. Wilber Broyles (has been remodeled)
15. George Vawter
16. Hans Creek Church
17. Charlie Ellison (Above where Robert and Gladys lived and raised their kids)
18. Addison Ellison's (Built around the original log house)
19. Remodeled and built on to old Lowe home where Kit Ballengee lives.
20. George Underwood (has been remodeled)
21. Rhym Mann (In front of Bobby Broyles. Burned)
22. Orchard Store (Torn down)
23. Plunk Miller (Where Lil and Gene lives. Plunk was a brother to J. C. Miller's wife, Lilly)
24. Lon Lively (Where Pearl Huddleson lived. Porch has been enclosed)
25. John Broyles   (Miller ? lives there now. It caught fire but has been restored)
26. Preacher Dunn (Where Howard Spencer lives)
27. Old Dunn Home by P. O. and Cashmere store
28. Marshell Dunn's (Between cashmere and Peterstown. He also built barn at that place. A windstorm blew it down but it was repaired and re-erected.

At Lindside
29. Old Ballard home where Madge Ballard lived
30. Built one up in the Valley from Lindside. Daddy helped wire it when electricity became available. I'm not sure where it is.
31. Broyles home where Aunt Catheryn lived on road from Lindside to Peterstown.
32. and 33. Two for Hansbarger on same road as Broyles. Ecol's and Will's. Ecol's caught fire but was restored. It was a big kinda long white house. Will's was the big house that Hall bought.
34. Colter Home. Where you turn to go to fish hatchery. It was torn down. Harry Allen built on the sight. Uncle Ray took the plainer over there with a team of horses. It took him all day. There wasn't any where to eat and they didn't offer him a thing to eat. Grandma never could stand them after that for letting Ray go hungry. (His name was Adare)
35. Schoolhouse in Peterstown. Torn down. Bank built on site.
36. Old E. I. Terry home. (It's been bricked over. In front of new Bank)
37. Dr. Hunter's home. Close to Funeral home
38. Dr. Hunter's Office

Old Dunn House. Where John and Carroll was born. Arthur Dean said someone else built this one.
40. E.I. Terry's store. remodeled
41. Old Bank at Peterstown, remodeled.
42. Old Heslep home, second house on cornor on St. beside the Bank.
43. Cliff Spangler. Big red brick on road that goes to the Orchard Addition
44. Clara Hines house, built for Dick Hines, Jess Hines' brother

BALLARD

45. Old Bivens home, Dink's dad.
46. Old Store. Biven's. Where P.O. was.
47. Living quarters to Ballard Food Center
48. Obie Broyles where Cleo lived. Burned
49. Red Sulphur Springs Church
50. Old Humphreys Store. Burned
51. Dr. Campbell's house. The big one beside the road to the church
52. Old Dr. Campbell's home on Red Sulphur Road that goes to Greenville. (Ralph Campbell)
53. Old Dunn Home He remodeled this one. Hallie Dickerson owned it
54. Peach Fleshman's old home. Torn down. Homer Long built on sight. Clark borned here.
55. Janie Shepp Fleshman Home. He jusst remodeled it. This is in back of Hallie Dickerson's This house was built for Dr. Will Hunter. (His Brother, Dr. John Hunter delivered Irene and Lilly)
56. Dr. Ryans home in Indian Mills. (He was a brother to Maude Lowe)
57. The Miller home where Fred Wesley lived. He built dining room, kitchen, front and back porches and bay windows. He also built the shop.
58. Old John Miller home, down in the Wesley hollow where Grnadma Fronie lived. All the Millers were born here. (Cal whitten owned it until his death) Torn down
59. Simm's Home. On another side road off 219 near Colter home. Toney's own it

He also built about 200 company house in Pageston and Welch for the N and W railroad. Burley Miller took Papa's team of horses, named Pete and Frank, with loaded wagon and drove through to these locations and sstayed and worked them until the job was finished. When they came back home, Frank was blind. Later Papa's old bull killed Frank one day when everyone was gone for the day. The next day Papa took the bull to Greenville and sold him to Jack Johnson.

Appendix B

No.	Early Owner	Loc.	Date	Style	Current Owners, (etc.)
1	Charlie M. Bivens	Cash.	1886	Vernac	Tammy Long
2	John R. Ryan	Orch.	1923	Q-An-A	(Burned)
3	Robert S. Dunlap	Green.		Folk-Vic	Rhonda Dortch
4	Issac N. Ballard	Green.		Folk-Vic	Eva M. Chandler
5	Robert H. Arnott	Green.	1905	Q-An-A	Howdy & Suzie Henritz
6	Long Store	Green.		Vernac	(Razed)
7	John Frank Maddy	Green.		Prairie	Brandon Smith
8	John R. Johnson	Green.	1907	Q-An-B	Layman & Laurie Thomas
9	Robert E. Riner	Ways.		Q-An-A	(Burned)
9A	Mary Jane Pence	Green.		Col-Rev	Otis Pence
10	George P. Young	Green.		Q-An-A	James & Deborah Ashley
11	Dewey E. Pence	Hans	1906	Q-An-A	James McGrady
12	Addison Dunlap	Hans	1913	remodel	Petrie D. Brown & siblings
13	Letcher E. Miller	Hans	1901	Q-An-A	(Razed)
14	Wilber L. Broyles	Hans		Q-An-A	(Razed)
15	George W. Vawter	Hans	1899	Folk-Vic	Robert Larew, Michael Lentz
16	Hans Creek Church	Hans	1912	Vernac	d.n.a.
17	Charles L. Ellison	Hans		Craft	Barbara E. Level & siblings
18	Addison D. Ellison	Hans	1873	remodel	Bert & Paula Ellison
19	Dorse E. Lowe	Orch.		remodel	(Razed)
20	George W. Underwood	Orch.		Q-An-A	(Changed beyond recognition)
21	Rhume C. Mann	Orch.		?	(Burned)
22	Orchard Store	Orch.		Vernac	(Razed)
23	Andrew P. Miller	Orch.		Shingle	Clark & Linda Humphreys
24	Leonidas Lively	Orch.		Q-An-B?	James Powell
25	John A. Broyles	Lins.		Q-An-A	Christy Reece
26	Arthur D. Dunn	Cash.		Q-An-A	Daniel Spencer
27	Ell Harold Dunn	Cash.		Q-An-B	Raymond Comer
28	Marshall B. Dunn	Cash.	1899	Q-An-A	Marshall L. & Frances Dunn
29	Mabel M. Ballard	Lins.		Craft	Alma L. Ballard
30	John A. McDaniel	Lins.		Folk-Vic	Roger & Becky Crabtree
31	Katheryn V. Dillon	Lins.		Q-An-A	Aaron & Alana Tony
32	William H. Hansbarger	Lins.		Q-An-A	Grover Jones
33	John Echols Hansbarger	Lins.		Folk-Vic	Mrs. George Todd heirs
34	John Henry Coulter	Lins.		Folk-Vic	(Razed)
35	Peterstown School	Peter.	1912	Richard	(Razed)
36	E.I. Terry	Peter.		Q-Anne	Jim & Jodie Posey
37	Dr. John O. Hunter	Peter.		Prairie	Ballard Investments
38	Dr. Hunter Office	Peter.		Craft	Stan Presley
39	Dunn	Peter.		Q-An-A	(Razed)

No.	Early Owner	Loc.	Date	Style	Current Owners, (etc.)
40	E.I. Terry	Peter.		Vernac?	(Razed)
41	Bank at Peterstown	Peter.		Vernac	(Razed)
42	Clarence O. Heslep	Peter.		Q-An-B	Robin A. Mann
43	Clifton M. Spangler	Peter.		Col-Rev	(Razed)
44	Charles Albert Hines	Cash.		Q-An-A	(Burned)
45	Frank C. Bivens	Ball.		Q-An-A	George W. Bostic
46	Bivens Store	Ball.		Folk-Vic	(Razed)
47	Ballard Food Center	Ball.		Vernac	(Burned)
48	Samuel O. Broyles	Ball.		Q-An-B	Billy & Melva Wheeler
49	Red S.S. Church	Red S.	1895	Vernac	d.n.a.
50	Humphreys Store	Red S.		Folk-Vic	(Burned)
51	Dr. Lewis M. Campbell	Red S.	1923	Vernac	Jack & Susan Parker
52	Charles W. Campbell	Red S.		Q-An-A	Ralph & Ardella Campbell
53	Charles L. Dunn	Red S.		remodel	Abner Kinsinger
54	Lewis A. Fleshman	Red S.		Q-An-A	(Razed)
55	Janie Sheppe Fleshman	Red S.		Craft	Julie & Rodney Bragg
56	Dr. Dorsey McN. Ryan	Indian		Q-An-A	Rusty Simmons
57	Fred Wesley	Hans		Folk-Vic	(Razed)
58	John C. Miller	Hans		Vernac	(Razed)
59	Clarence V. Symns	Lins.		Q-An-B	Lacy & Jaquetta Toney

References

Allison, R. L. (2013). *Brownie Barked at Midnight*.

American Architect and Building News (Vol. 1-90), (1876).

Ancestry.com (n.d.). http://Ancestry.com

Attend Funeral. (1965, March 24). *Beckley Post-Herald*. (Dr. Green's services p. 7)

Ballard, M. B. (1957). *William Ballard*. Privately published.

Ballard, M. B. (1969, Jan. 23.) Correspondence Re: Red Sulphur Springs (1890-1891) *The Monroe Watchman*. (p. 2)

Bank's President Retires After 25 Years of Service. (1973, August 20). *Beckley Post Herald*. (Dunlap news p. 8)

Barber, G. F. (2008). *Barber's Turn-of-the-Century Houses* (3rd ed.). Courier Corporation.

Bicentennial Committee, M. C. (1997). *Highlights of the History of Monroe County Schools 1799-1999*. Monroe County Bicentennial Committee.

C. M. Bivens, 72, Dies In Hospital. (1964, September 30). *Beckley Post-Herald*. (Obituary p. 15)

Cirker, B. (1996). *Victorian House Designs in Authentic Full Color*. Courier Corporation.

Classified Ads. (1947, July 18). *Beckley Post-Herald*. (Locust Hall sale of bulls p. 14)

Cohen, S. (1981). *Historic Springs of the Virginias*. Pictorial Histories Publishing Co., Charleston, West Virginia.

Company, R. (1990). *Sears, Roebuck Home Builder's Catalog* (1910 reprint). Dover Publishing, Inc.

Comstock, J. F. (1974). *The West Virginia Heritage Encyclopedia* (p. 3020).

Comstock, W. T. (1893). *Turn-of-the-Century House Designs*. Dover Publications Inc.

Comstock, W. T. (2012). *Victorian Domestic Architectural Plans and Details* (Reprint: original from 1988). Dover Publications Inc.

Comstock, W. T. (2013). *Late Victorian Architectural Plans and Details 1888-1890*. Dover Publications Inc.

C.W. Campbell Is Taken At 79. (1935, March 22). *Charleston Daily Mail*. (Obituary p. 1)

Czompo, E. H. (2011). *Memories of Hans Creek.* Self-published.

DAR Members Plan Centennial Observance. (1956, June 24). *Beckley Post-Herald.* (Locust Hall [Hansbarger] entertaining p. 4)

Davis, S. M. (1931, June 28). Peterstown News. *Bluefield Daily Telegraph.* (Heslep and Hansbarger personals p. 8)

Delia S. Heslep Succumbs At 84. (1963, September 24). *Beckley Post-Herald.* (Obituary p. 9)

Donnelly, S. (1956, July 17). Ray S. Miller Cited For Invention. *Beckley Post-Herald.* (p. 4)

Dr. Adair Rites. (1950, March 5). *Newspapers.Com.* (Obituary p.1 and 13)

Dr. John O. Hunter. (1963, May 19). *Beckley Post-Herald/Raleigh Register.* (Obituary p. 2)

Dr. Ryan's Rites to be Saturday. (1945, September 21). *Beckley Post-Herald.* (Obituary p. 12)

Dumont, J. W. (1987). *Red Sulphur Springs Background Survey Report.* (Manuscript located in Caperton Museum, Union, West Virginia)

Dunlap, Charles B. (1976). Untitled, unpublished manuscript written for Harriet Ellison Dobbs, owner of the Dunlap home. Property of Petrie Brown.

Dunn, V. and C. (1987). *Our Time in History 1758-1987: Descendants of John Dunn and Mary Peters* (p. 151). South Daytona Instant Print.

E.A. Hansbarger Dies, Statehouse Employee Since '33. (1961, March 9). *Charleston Daily Mail.* (Obituary p. 39)

Evans, M.P. (2009). *The Country Store and the Earache Cure, Coal Camps and Castor Oil: Tales from the Good Old Days in Southern West Virginia.* Hometown Memories Publishing Co.

Fifty Years Ago. (1951, December 13). *The Monroe Watchman.* (Letcher Miller house construction 1901 p. 7)

Fifty Years Ago. (1952, July 17). *The Monroe Watchman.* (Humphreys Store built in 1901 p. 7)

Find-a-Grave.com (n.d.). http://find-a-grave.com

Fleshman, M. K. (2003). *Jacob Mann, Jr.: Early Pioneer of Monroe County, West Virginia and his Descendants.* Gateway Press, Inc.

Fleshman, R. F., & Clark, B. L. (n.d.). *Christian Peters & Peterstown Community, Monroe County, West Virginia* (pp. 24–25). (Typed manuscript)

Fleshner, H. (1954). Craftsman, 90, Going Strong. *Huntington Herald-Dispatch..*

Former Monroe Resident Marks 90th Anniversary. (1954, August 27). *Beckley Post-Herald*. (John Campbell Miller event p. 24)

Former Pastor Expresses Surprise at City's Growth. (1936, August 18). *Bluefield Daily Telegraph*. (Will Hansbarger's marriage p. 10)

Goreman, J. L., & Newman, L. S. (1965). *Soil Survey of Monroe County, West Virginia* (Series 1960. No. 23). U.S. Dept. of Agriculture.

Greenville Gets Hardware Store. (1949, October 10). *Beckley Post-Herald*. (Dunlap news p. 12)

Hardesty. (2010). *Monroe County, West Virginia: History and Biographies* (Reprinted from 1883 original). Mountain Press.

Haworth, J. R. (1956). Carpenter, 92, Works Daily. *Huntington Herald-Dispatch*.

Howdock, P., Editor. (1999). *Your Heritage* (Bicentennial, pp. 2, 15, 17). Friends & Neighbors Club.

Ideal Summer Home: Come to Monroe County, West Virginia. (1894). *The Monroe Watchman*. (Tourist brochure)

John Frank Maddy. (1935, January 11). *The News Leader (Staunton, Virginia)*. (Obituary p. 2)

Library, Virginia State. (1917). *Report of the Virginia State Library* (Vol. 13-14, p. 399). Register of the General Assembly of VA. (Wilson Lively)

Man Crushed to Death In Mercer Truck Crash. (1963, September 26). *Beckley Post-Herald*. (Kenny Coulter death p. 19])

Martindale, L. (2017). *Highways to Health and Pleasure: The Antebellum Turnpikes and Trade of the Mineral Springs in Greenbrier and Monroe Counties, Virginia* (Reprint). Monroe County Historical Society.

Mattie Johnson Succumbs At 72. (1968, July 1). *Beckley Post-Herald*. (Obituary p. 10)

McAlester, V. S. (2018). *A Field Guide to American Houses*. Knopf.

Miss Bivens' Funeral Set. (1975, February 12). *Beckley Post-Herald*.

Monroe County Land Transfers. (1969, December 6). *Beckley Post-Herald*. (Locust Hall business p. 16)

Monroe Men: John Campbell Miller File (Collection of clippings). (n.d.). (Caperton Museum, Back room, Shelf Unit "C". Shelf 2)

Monroe Town Was[n't] Named for Christian Peters in 1784. (1975, August 2). *Beckley Post-Herald/Raleigh Register*. (E.I. Terry store p. 67)

Morton, O. F. (1916). *A History of Monroe County, West Virginia*. The McClure Company, Inc.

Mrs. Hansbarger, Peterstown, Dies. (1954, August 15). *Beckley Post-Herald/Raleigh Register*. (p. 1)

Mrs. L. A. Fleshman. (1953, September 9). *The News Leader (Staunton, Virginia)* (Obituary p. 14)

Mrs. Zula S. Maddy. (1962, August 28). *The News Leader (Staunton, Virginia)*. (Obituary p. 2)

National Bank of Peterstown, T. F. (2010). *100 Year Anniversary Calendar. Newspapers.com (no date)* http://newspapers.com

Noe, K. W. (1994). *Southwest Virginia's Railroad: Modernization and the Sectional Crisis in the Civil War Era*. University of Alabama Press.

Performs Unusual Operation. (1925, April 5). *Bluefield Daily Telegraph*. (Sheppe event p. 29)

Personals. (1931, June 28). *Bluefield Daily Telegraph*. (Locust Hall [Hansbargers] entertaining p. 8)

Personals. (1931, July 26). *Bluefield Telegraph*. (Locust Hall [Hansbargers] entertaining p. 4)

Peterstown Founded Shortly Before 1800. (1931, October 29). *Bluefield Daily Telegraph*. (photo, bank presidents p. 12)

Peterstown News. (1949, July 11). *Beckley Post-Herald*. (Dr. R. J. Sheppe locates dentist practice p. 2)

Peterstown Now A Modern Village. (1931, October 29). *Bluefield Daily Telegraph*. C. O. Heslep, (Miller information and photo of Heslep Mill p. 14)

Reiff, D. D. (2000). *Houses from Books: Treatises, Pattern Books, and Catalog in American Architecture: 1738-1950: A History and Guide*. Penn State Press.

Ripley, R., Banks, J., & Allen, J. H. (2000). *The History of Greenville* (pp. 13–19). Monroe County Historical Society. (Caperton Museum, Union, West Virginia)

Rites Incomplete for Mrs. Dillon. (1970, February 18). *Beckley Post-Herald*. (Katheryn Miller Dillon obituary p. 9)

Reger, D. B., & Price, P. H. (1926). *West Virginia Geological Survey: Mercer, Monroe, and Summers Counties*. Wheeling News Litho. Co.

Rossiter, E. & Wright, F. (1883, illustrated 2001). *Authentic Color Schemes for Victorian Houses* (Reprint). Dover Publications, Inc.

Schroeder, Jr., J. J. (1969). *Sears Roebuck & Co. 1908 Catalog* (No. 117). The Gun Digest Co.

Sears Modern Homes, (reprint of 1913 edition). (2006). Dover Publishing.

Sears Roebuck Builder's Hardware and Materials Catalog (pp. 100–110). (1897). Skyhorse Publishing.

Sears Roebuck Catalog (No. 117). (1908). Gun Digest Co.

Sears, Roebuck Home Builder's Catalog (reprint of 1910). (1990). Dover Publications.

Shumate, H. D., Banks, M. N., Shumate, K. G., & Banks, J. W. (1990). *Cemeteries of Monroe County, West Virginia.* The Monroe Watchman for the Monroe County Historical Society. (Caperton Museum, Union, West Virginia)

Stickley, G. (1988). *Craftsman Bungalows.* Dover Publishing.

Survey Finished on Tile Drainage. (1955, July 10). *Beckley Post-Herald/Raleigh Register.* (Locust Hall business p. 10)

Thirty Years Ago. (1952, December 11). *The Monroe Watchman.* (Dr. Campbell bought lot from O. L. Heslep p. 7)

Thomas Crotshin Taken by Death. (1949, October 10). *Beckley Post Herald.* (Obituary p. 12)

Trout, W. E. (2003). *The New River Atlas.* Virginia Canals and Navigation Society.

Two Charged With Stealing After A Fire. (1937, June 6). *Raleigh Register.* (Terry store p. 6)

W. Churchill's Daughter Is Guest at Home of Monroe County Man. (1966, December 28). *Beckley Post-Herald.* (Pete Ballard event p. 10)

West Virginia Legislative Hand Book and Manual and Official Register. (1917) Compiled and Edited by John T. Harris, Clerk of the Senate, The Tribune Printing Co., Charleston, West Va. (pgs. 719 - 770)

Young, N. (1994, Nov. 28). Healing Powers. *Beckley Register Herald.* (Red Sulphur Springs)

Ziegler, F. (2019). *The Settlement of the Greater Greenbrier Valley, West Virginia.* 35th Star Publishing.

Note: References not specifically cited were used as a source of general information or to confirm date.

Notes

Introduction

1. Ziegler, "Settlement of the Greater Greenbrier Valley."

Chapter One

2. Haworth, "Carpenter, 92, Works Daily."
3. Rossiter & Wright, "Authentic Color Schemes for Victorian Houses."
4. Noe, "Southwestern Virginia's Railroad."
5. Reger and Price, "West Virginia Geological Survey," 23.

Chapter Two

6. Ziegler, "Settlement of the Greater Greenbrier Valley."
7. Ripley and Allen, "History of Greenville," 13-19.
8. Ballard, "William Ballard."
9. Evans, "The Country Store."

Chapter Three

10. Martindale, "Highways to Health."
11. Dunlap, Untitled manuscript.
12. Martindale, "Highways to Health."
13. Dunlap, Untitled manuscript.
14. Czompo, "Memories of Hans Creek."
15. Ellison & Parkinson, 1980.
16. Ellison and Parkinson, "The Ellisons of Hans Creek," 56-64.

Chapter Five

17. Beckley Post-Herald, June 24, 1956. "DAR Members Plan Centennial." Beckley Post-Herald July 18, 1947. "Classified Ads."

18. Harris, "West Virginia Legislative Handbook," 719-770.

Chapter Six

19. Cohen, "Historic Springs."

20. Beckley Post-Herald/Raleigh Register, May 19, 1963 "Dr. John O. Hunter," 2.

21. Beckley Post-Herald, December 28, 1966, "Winston Churchill's Daughter Is Guest," 10.

22. Beckley Post-Herald/Raleigh Register, August 2, 1975, "Monroe Town Was[n't] Named," 67.

23. Raleigh Register, June 6, 1937. "Two Charged With Stealing," 6.

Chapter Seven

24. Morton, "History of Monroe County."

25. Dunn V. and C., "Our Time in History," 151.

Chapter Eight

26. Dumont, "Red Sulphur Springs Background."

27. Ibid.

28. Cohen, "Historic Springs of Virginias."

29. Ballard, "William Ballard."

30. Young, Beckley Register Herald, Nov. 28, 1994, "Healing Powers."

31. Dumont, "Red Sulphur."

32. Howdock. "Your Heritage."

NOTES

Index

A

Adair Ridge Road 144
Aladdin Company 7
Allegheny Mountains 1
Allen, Christina Dillow 107
Allen, Harry 92, 107
Allison, Roberta Larew 55
American Revolution 21, 45
Anderson, Sharon 30
Appalachian Mountains 2
Arnott, Jane Robinson Bittinger (Janie) 29
Arnott, Robert Handley (Bub) 26, 29, 41
Ashley, James and Deborah 42

B

Ballard & Arnott Mercantile 32
Ballard & Arnott Store 26
Ballard & Thomas Store 26, 30
Ballard Baptist Church 129, 133, 145
Ballard Christian School 133
Ballard Food Center 80, 129, 142
Ballard Investments LLC 115
Ballard Store 93
Ballard-Red Sulphur Parkway 131, 134-35, 138, 142, 153
Ballard, Alma Louise (Lou) 93
Ballard, Arthur J. (Pete) 115
Ballard, Benny Curtis 93
Ballard, Clarence A. 93
Ballard, Clarence Eugene 93
Ballard, Clayton 129
Ballard, Garnet Clay 93
Ballard, Glenn Chambers 93
Ballard, Herbert Clark 93
Ballard, Issac Newton (Ike) 22, 26, 29-30
Ballard, James Claude 93
Ballard, Kate May Walkup 22, 26
Ballard, Mabel May Broyles (Madge) 93
Ballard, Maggie 22, 26, 115, 161
Ballard, Thomas Calvin 93
Ballard, Thomas, & Co. 26
Ballard, Wade H., II (Colonel 126
Ballard, Wade H., III (Jim) 115
Ballard, West Virginia 14, 57, 78, 81, 129, 130, 140-42, 144-45, 153-4
Ballengee, Kit 78, 150
Ballengee, Neva 150
Baltimore 11, 101
Beasley, George 155
Beirne, Andrew 49
Belcher, Dennis Mason 138
Biggs, Thomas J. and Sarah, J. 158
Bittinger, Rev. M. H. 29
Bivens, Callie Rosetta 141
Bivens, Charlie M. 131
Bivens, Clara Josephine Ballard 140
Bivens, Elaine Ruth 141
Bivens, Evelyn Jeanette Ward 141
Bivens, Everette Duane 141
Bivens, Frank Commodore 140-1
Bivens, Frank Commodore, Jr. 141
Bivens, Gladys S. 141
Bivens, Howard Hunter 141
Bivens, Hyla Johnson 141
Bivens, Vivian Rose 141
Bivens, William Oren (Dink) 141
Blankenship, Nannie Lula Lively 87
Blue Sulphur Springs 149
Blue Sulphur Turnpike 14, 49
Bluefield Daily Telegraph 114, 118
Bluestone Dam 147, 150, 160
Bluestone River 14
Boone, John 92
Bostic, George W. 141
Braden, Grace Glenna Pence 46
Bragg, Julie and Rodney 161
Brown, Mae Heslep 131
Brown, Samuel Roy (Sonny), Jr. 131
Brown, Samuel Roy Sr. 131
Broyles Cemetery Road 92
Broyles, Franklin Dale 145
Broyles, Garnet Julian (Bus) 144-5
Broyles, George Finley (Finn) 144

Broyles, Gladys Lynch 55, 61
Broyles, Helen Mae 55
Broyles, Ida Katherine 55
Broyles, John Alexander 92
Broyles, Mahala Etta McDaniel 92
Broyles, Maud Smith 144
Broyles, Minnie B. Crotty 144
Broyles, Nora Lee Lane 143
Broyles, Otis Christopher 55
Broyles, Pat 80, 143
Broyles, Roy Edwin 55
Broyles, Samuel Overton 144
Broyles, Stanley Crotty 144
Broyles, Wilbur Lee 55
Brush Creek 2, 129
Buckland, J. B. 92, 138

C

C. O. Heslep Milling 122
Caine, Frances L. Dunn 134
Calloway, Alice 53
Campbell, Ardella Long (Tootie) 158
Campbell, Charles William (C. W.) 150, 154, 157
Campbell, Frank 55
Campbell, Isaac 155, 158
Campbell, Lewis McClure (L. M.) 7, 150, 154-55, 157
Campbell, Mary Catherine Johnson 157
Campbell, Ralph 158
Campbell, Rebecca Jane 5
Campbell, Robert Dunbar 157
Canterbury, Annie Evelyn McDaniel 95
Carpenter, John, 5, 13
Carter, Mary J. Lively 87
Cashmere, West Virginia 14, 129, 130, 133, 134-35, 138
Centreville 21
Chandler, Eva May 26
Chandler, Thomas Ballard 26
Chapman's Battery, Confederate States of America 5
Chesapeake and Ohio Railroad 13
Churchill, Sarah 115
Churchill, Winston 115
Cirker, Blanche 172
Civil War 5, 6, 13, 41, 54, 15
Clark, Helen Houston Ballard 22
Clark, Helen Houston Ballard 26
Clark's Mill 122

Classical Revival style 49
Coalter, Marjorie Brown McDaniel 95
Cody, Glenna Lucille Johnson 35
Collins, Anna Rebecca Maddy 33
Colonial Revival 6, 9, 39, 126
Comer, Lucy Toney 108
Comstock, William T. 7
Cook, Valentine 2
Cooks Fort 21, 35
Cooks Mill 21, 35
Cooks Old Mill 3
Coulter, Emaline Ellison 106
Coulter, Eva Blair 107
Coulter, John Henry 106
Coulter, John Odie 93
Coulter, Kenny Ray 93, 106
Crabtree, Roger and Becky 95
Craftsman style 1, 6, 11, 63, 77, 93, 115, 161
Crotshin, Robert 153
Czompo, Elizabeth Hines 57, 61

D

Dent, Bethel 122
Dent, Walter and Annie 122
Devere, Dan 61
Diamond Lew 154
Dickinson, Hallie 160
Dickison, Guy 161
Dillion, Hugh C. 92
Dillion, Pearl Mae Broyles 92
Dillon, Katheryn Virginia Miller 70, 100
Dobbs, Harriet Petrie Ellison (see also Ellison, Harriet Petrie Dunlap) 50-51
Dobbs, Lee Filmore 50
Dobbs, Samantha 55
Dortch, Rhonda 22
Dry Pond 80, 138
Dunlap, Addison (1801-1870) 49-50
Dunlap, Alexander 49
Dunlap, Charles B. (1910) 49-50
Dunlap, Charles H. (1839-1904) 49
Dunlap, Clara Petrie 49
Dunlap, Edward Patterson (Pat) 22
Dunlap, Elizabeth Patterson 22
Dunlap, Elsie Nason (Deedie) 50
Dunlap, Frances McElheney 49
Dunlap, Isaac Campbell 49
Dunlap, James A. (1799-1843) 49
Dunlap, James 49

Dunlap, Jane. A. 49-50
Dunlap, Marion Addison 22
Dunlap, Martha Smart Bates 50
Dunlap, Robert Smart (Bert) 22
Dunlap, William P. (Billie) 50
Dunn, Anna Clay 136
Dunn, Arthur Dean 133
Dunn, Arthur Dean, Jr. 133
Dunn, Catherine Julia Ballard 93, 135, 159
Dunn, Charles Lewis 159
Dunn, Daisy Florence 133
Dunn, Eli Harold 134
Dunn, Emmett Delford 136
Dunn, Euna Lee 136
Dunn, Eva Cordelia McClelland 134
Dunn, Gladys Campbell 136
Dunn, Harry Hobart 136
Dunn, James C. 135
Dunn, James Martin 135
Dunn, John 135
Dunn, Joseph Harold 134
Dunn, Lelia Gertrude 135-36
Dunn, Lewis Allen 135
Dunn, Louisa Jane Spangler 159
Dunn, Mabel Carrington 136
Dunn, Marshall Burlington 135-36
Dunn, Marshall Lee 136
Dunn, Mary Frances South 136
Dunn, Mary Kathleen Johnson (Thummie) 35
Dunn, Mary Peters 135
Dunn, Miriam Katherine 136
Dunn, Nancy Louisa 133
Dunn, Nellie Blaine 136
Dunn, Quentin Telford 136
Dunn, Vernon 135, 159
Dunn, Zula McClelland 134

E

E. I. Terry Store 114, 118
Elkhorn West Virginia 167
Ellison, Addison Dunlap 64
Ellison, Alpha Broyles 64
Ellison, Anne English 64
Ellison, Bert 65
Ellison, Charles Alexander 63
Ellison, Charles L. 63
Ellison, Charley and Dolly 81
Ellison, Earl 153
Ellison, Emma Catherine Kyle 64
Ellison, Frances Bailey Waters 63
Ellison, Harriet Petrie Dunlap (see also Dobbs, Harriet Petrie Ellison) 49, 64-65
Ellison, Helen Steele 65
Ellison, James 64
Ellison, Jesse 64
Ellison, John Zachariah (1840-1934) 50, 64
Ellison, John Zachariah (Zack the second) 64-65
Ellison, Juliet (Judy) Ellen Kuhn 46, 65
Ellison, Mary E. 100
Ellison, Paula 66
Ellison, Richard Warren 65
Ellison, Zachariah 64
Ellison's Ridge Road 21
Evans, Alexander 100
Evans, Alfred 100
Evans, Catherine Raines (Kate) 100
Evans, Marshalene Pence 32-3
Evans, Paul A. 100
Evans, Roena J. Epperly 100
Evans, Samuel F. 100

F

Farley, Burnice Dee 147
Farley, Charles Mark 147
Farley, Ethel May Shepard 147
Farm Heritage Trail 14
Fayette Turnpike 14, 111
Ferrell, Anna Clayton Bivens 141
First National Bank of Peterstown 103, 108, 112, 114, 120
Fischmann, Alma Gertrude Johnson Grey Morgan 35
Fitz Valley 149
Fleshman, Ida Dillon 147
Fleshman, Jenneta Armstrong Sheppe (Janie) 161
Fleshman, Lewis Allen (Teets) 161
Fleshman, William Adair 147
Fletcher, Ruth E. Dunn 133
Forest Hill, West Virginia 163
Fountain Springs 14, 91, 101, 105-6
Four-Square style 11, 33, 115
Francis, Elizabeth Ann Farley 147
Francis, Tom 147

Frazier, Minnie Pearl Calloway Broyles 55
Freshour, Mabel Lura Ryan 78

G

Gap Mills, West Virginia 105-6
George F. Barber & Co. 7
Giles Turnpike 14, 111
Glen Lyn, Virginia 13, 107
Gothic style 8, 9, 61
Gray Sulphur Springs 11, 111
Green, Thomas Campbell 93
Greenbrier County, West Virginia 5, 159
Greenbrier River 14, 150
Greene, Irene Wesley 13, 46, 74, 147, 175
Greene, Johnny 13, 175
Greenville, West Virginia 14, 21-22, 26, 29, 32-35, 39, 41-42, 46, 54-55, 57, 115

H

Hale, Carrie A. 106
Halstead, David 57
Halstead, Davis A. 8
Hans Creek Church 61
Hans Creek Road 50
Hans Creek Valley, West Virginia 5, 14, 45-6, 49-50, 54-55, 57, 61, 64-65, 77-78, 143
Hans Creek 1, 2, 41, 45
Hansbarger, Anna Salomi Peery 101
Hansbarger, Charles (Charley) Jacob 106
Hansbarger, Clark 105
Hansbarger, Evelyn 105-6
Hansbarger, John Echols 101, 103, 105
Hansbarger, John Hill 101
Hansbarger, Julia Lee 103
Hansbarger, Lilly Mandan Lively 101
Hansbarger, Madge 101
Hansbarger, Susan Neel 98
Hansbarger, Thomas Frederick 101
Hansbarger, William Henry 101, 106
Hardesty, H. H. 103
Harvey Mann General Store 143
Harvey, James 159
Harvey, Melvin and Vivian 92
Harvey, Nicholas 159

Helvey, Bill 155
Henderson, John 54
Hendrick, Frances Ellison 63
Henritz, Howdy and Suzie 30
Heslep, Alena May Keatley 122
Heslep, Clarence Oren 122
Heslep, James 122
Heslep, Joseph 122
Heslep, Lucille 122
Heslep, Otis (Otuse) 8, 154
Heslep, Virginia 122
Hines, Anise Alderson 138
Hines, Annie Luther Hale 138
Hines, Charles Albert 138
Hines, Charles Oscar 138
Hines, Clara Belcher Spangler 138
Hines, Dennis Hale 138
Hines, Luther Julian 138
Hines, Oat 61
Hines, Sarah Josephine Vawter 57
Hinton, West Virginia 26, 150, 163,
Hodge, Eva 143
Hodges, Billy 161
Holsambak, Alva Irene McDaniel 95
Huddleston, John and Pearl 87
Humphrey's Store 153
Humphreys, Alex 144
Humphreys, Clark 13, 82
Humphreys, Lilly Katherine Wesley 46, 74, 82
Humphreys, Linda 13, 82
Humphreys, Samuel (Gene) 83
Hunt, Julia Patterson 22
Hunter, John Oscar 111, 115, 133
Hunter, Myrtle Geneva Fleshman 115
Hunter, William Lester 115, 161
Huntington, West Virginia 1, 5, 7, 70, 157

I

Indian 14, 21, 111
Indian Creek 2, 14, 21-2, 34, 39, 41-2, 45, 77, 149-50, 153, 157, 163
Indian Mills, West Virginia 149-50, 161, 163
Indian Mills Road 161, 163
Ireland (Irish) 55, 78

J

Jackson River 13
James River Valley 1
Johnson, Ellen Spangler 126, 153
Johnson, Georgia Young 35
Johnson, Jack Jr. (Eddie) 35
Johnson, John Edwin 35
Johnson, John Robert (Jack) 8, 35, 55
Johnson, Mattie Reeves Brown 35
Johnson, William Robert 35
Jones, Donnie and Patty 143
Jones, Grover 101
Jones, Murph 129

K

Kanawha Turnpike 14, 111
Keatley, Lennie 5
Keffler, Nina Ellen Bivens 141
Key, Francis Scott 150
Kibble Hill 44, 57, 78, 80, 163
Kinsinger, Abner 160

L

Lane, Lonnie and Elizator 143
Larew, Robert 57
Laurel Creek 21
Lawhorn, Irene 100
Lawhorn, Ralph Monroe 34
Lawhorn, Ruby Lee Mann 34
Lee, Robert E. 64, 87
Lentz, Michael 57
Lester, Gary 131
Lester, Tom 131
Levandowski, Cathy McDaniel 95
Level, Barbara Ellison 63
Lindside, West Virginia 14, 77, 87, 91, 93, 100, 103, 107
Lively, Charles Spurgeon 87
Lively, Corlelia Graydon 87
Lively, Cornelius Wilson 87
Lively, Cottrell 87
Lively, George William 87
Lively, Leonidas Marion (Lon) 87-88
Lively, Lillie Pleasant Hoke 87
Lively, Omar Talmage 87
Lively, Opie Dorsey 87
Locust Hall Farm Company 103
Long, Allen Madison 33, 158
Long, Ernest Weldon 158
Long, Homer 161
Long, Nellie Gray Ballard 158
Long, Oral Jefferson 158
Long, Orville Milton (Shorty) 33
Long, Otis 33
Long, Reba Saunders 33
Long, Sarah Ardella Lawrence 158
Long, Tammy 131
Long's Store 31
Lord Dunmore's War 21
Lowe, Dorse E. 78
Lowe, Maude Ryan 79, 163
Lowell, West Virginia 13, 40, 150
Lowry, Jennifer 42

M

Maddy, Frank 32, 33
Maddy, Ruth Elinor 33
Maddy, Ruth H. McDaniel 95
Maddy, Zula Gertrude Shirey 33
Maddy's Store 32
Mann-Ballard & Co. Store 93
Mann, Anna Ethel Johnson 35
Mann, Harvey 143
Mann, Paula Oliver 143
Mann, Paxton 142
Mann, Robin A. 122
Martin, Trixie 150
Matthews, Alexander F. 147
McAlester, Virginia Savage 8
McBride, Richard 143
McDaniel, Andrew Cecil 95
McDaniel, Andrew Pate 95
McDaniel, Everett Lee 95
McDaniel, John A. 94-5
McDaniel, Marshall 95
McDaniel, Mary Ann Humphreys 95
McDaniel, Opie Eldridge 95
McDaniel, Sarah Belle McGhee 95
McDaniel, Sherman Pate 95
McDowell County 7, 167
McGrady, James 46
McKenzie, Nally Wilson 126
Meadows, Bill and Bea Green 131
Mercer Anglers Club 95
Mill House 63
Miller, Adison Plunket (Plunk) 77, 82
Miller, Andrew P. 83
Miller, Arthur Dean 45

Miller, Avery 90
Miller, Burley 167
Miller, Charles L. 26
Miller, Dorsey Gordon 70
Miller, George Dewey 70
Miller, Henry, Sr. 95
Miller, John Campbell
   church construction: 61, 150
   era: 111, 129, 150, 171
   family: 1, 5, 13, 46, 70, 74, 82, 95, 100
   furniture: 82, 150
   house construction: 1-2, 5-9, 11, 13, 21, 29, 38, 46, 54, 57, 77-8, 82, 87, 93, 131, 150, 150, 157, 161, 163, 167
   house locations: 13-14, 45, 106, 111, 172
   physical description: 5
   remodeling: 39, 50, 64, 70, 118, 120, 159
   schools and stores: 111, 140, 150, 154
   styles: 17-19, 78, 82, 87, 130, 142
Miller, John Clyde 70
Miller, Letcher E. (Letch) 54
Miller, Lillie Belle 1, 46, 70, 82
Miller, Minnie Ballard 54
Miller, Ray Saleska 70
Miller, Rhoda Brooking 95
Miller, Roxie Campbell 150, 155
Miller, Sam 45
Miller, William F. 54
Miller, Wilson Mann 5, 95
Minter Homes Corporation 7
Mitchell, Katherine D. 103
Mohler, Craig 161
Monroe County, West Virginia
   Court: 93, 138
   Commission: 101
   description/history: 1- 2, 11, 91, 103, 111, 129, 153
   doctor: 133
   Miller family: 5-6, 171
   musicians: 131
   sheriff: 87
   Stockmen: 138
   store: 114, 118
   teachers: 35, 134, 161
Monroe County (West Virginia) Historical Society 7, 13, 174
Morton's History of Monroe County 153

N

Native American 1, 7
Neel, Richard Franklin 39
New Orleans 11
New River 1, 13, 111, 147, 150, 159-60
New York 7, 14, 131, 149
Newkirk, Craig 42
Nolan, Ora Jeanous Keatley Heslep 122
Norfolk & Western Railroad 13, 111, 167

O

Opportunity Knocks 115
Orchard Store 77, 81

P

Pageton, West Virginia 167
Painter Run Road 91, 107
Parker, Jack and Susan 155
Parkinson, George 65
Patterson, Marion 22
Patton, John Porter 105-6
Peck, Leona Lively 87
Pence, Dewey Edwin 39, 46, 65
Pence, Ella Marietta Arnott 46
Pence, Eva Mae Harvey 32
Pence, Forest D. 32
Pence, Kathern McDaniel (Kate) 95
Pence, Lewis Alexander 39, 40, 46
Pence, Maggie Gray 46
Pence, Mary Jane Neel 39-40, 46
Pence, Otis 39-40
Peters Mountain 2, 91, 94, 108
Peters, Christian 108
Peterstown Milling Co. 122
Peterstown Postmasters 70, 126
Peterstown Preservation Group 118
Peterstown School 9, 111-12, 138
Peterstown Town Council 122
Peterstown, West Virginia
   bank: 101, 103, 108, 114, 120, 147
   doctor: 115
   Eastern Star: 122
   economy: 11, 13, 114, 129
   growth: 91, 171
   history: 108, 111-12, 126, 147
   house locations: 14, 101, 114-15, 122, 126, 135

Philadelphia 8, 9, 11
Phipps, Sarah Elizabeth Sally Johnson 35
Pickaway, West Virginia 157
Pine Grove Road 14, 77, 80-82, 147
Posey, Jim and Jodie 114
Powell, Pat (Mrs. James) 88
Powers, Julia Reed Symns 108
Prairie style 9, 33, 115

Q

Queen Anne style 1, 8-9, 11, 26, 29, 33-34, 38, 41, 46, 54-55, 61, 87 92, 100-1, 103, 107, 122, 130, 135, 138, 140, 144, 157, 163, 171-72

R

Radford, Virginia 13
Red Sulphur Springs Church 150
Red Sulphur Springs Post Office 153
Red Sulphur Springs Resort 11, 13, 40, 49, 153, 155
Red Sulphur Springs, West Virginia 5, 14, 43, 49, 77-8, 115, 129, 149-50, 153-54, 157, 159, 161, 163
Red Sulphur Turnpike 13-14, 49
Redmond, Bill 160
Reece, Sam and Christy 92
Reiff, Daniel D. 6
Rich Creek, Virginia 103, 108, 111, 122, 129, 142
Rich Creek Valley 91
Riley, Stella Mae Broyles 144
Riner, Ann Keatley 78
Riner, Ethel Boon 38
Riner, Mary Pyne 78
Riner, John Thompson 38, 78
Riner, Robert, E. 38
Riner, Sarah H. Green 38
Riner, William C. 38, 78
Ripley, Ronald 105
Roles, Linda 160
Roosevelt, Theodore (Teddy) 144
Rossiter, Ehrick 8
Ryan, Dorsey McNeil (McNeelas) 163
Ryan, Elizabeth Mann 163
Ryan, Emma Bell 78
Ryan, Eunice Lois Lively 87
Ryan, Henry A. 78

Ryan, Martha Ellen Mann 78
Ryan, Norman 78
Ryan, Prince Edward 78
Ryan, Rosetta M. 78
Ryan, Thelma Inez Rose 163
Ryan, Wilbur L. 78
Ryan, William Francis 163
Ryan, John Richard (Johnny) 77-8

S

Salt Sulphur Springs Resort 11, 149
Salt Sulphur Turnpike 14
Scotland 54, 74
Sears (Roebuck & Co.) 6-8, 34, 115
Seneca Trail 14, 91, 93, 103
Shanklin, Robert and Rachel 21
Shanklin, Tom 29
Sheppe, Robert 161
Simmons, Rusty 163
Smith, Brandon 34
Smith, Erica and Mike 34
Smith, Minnie Clark Lively 87
Spangler, Anna Mae Ballard 93
Spangler, Annie Clark (Kate) 126
Spangler, Clifton Marshall 126
Spangler, Ellen Byrnside 126
Spangler, Everette Morris 126
Spangler, Florence Elizabeth 126
Spangler, Fred Clark 126
Spangler, H. Booker 126
Spangler, Leonard 92
Spangler, Lewis Clark (Bus) 126
Spangler, Mary L. 126
Spangler, Pansy C. 126
Spangler, Rosa Lee Broyles 92
Spangler, Wade (Shug) 159
Spencer, Daniel 133
Spencer, Lorraine Ingram 133
Spencer, Rev. James Howard Sr. 133
Spencer, Timothy 133
Stickley, Gustav 11
Sugar Run 45
Sweet Springs, West Virginia 11, 14, 149
Symns, Clarence Vincent 107-8
Symns, Clarence Vincent, Jr. 107-8
Symns, Elizabeth Peters (Betsie) 108
Symns, Evelyn Bane 108
Symns, John 10
Symns, Nancy Bane Adair (Nannie) 108
Symns, Samuel Young, II 108

T

Talcott, West Virginia 22, 163
Terry, Aaron and Alana 100
Terry, Annie C. Johnston 114
Terry, E. I. 110, 114
Thomas, Laurie Dobbs 35, 55
Thomas, Layman 35, 55
Thompson, Danny 30
Thompson, Norman 144
Timberlake, Robert W. 163
Todd, Mrs. George 10
Toney, Lacy and Jacquetta 108
Tygart River 14

U

Underwood, Eliza S. Miller 80
Underwood, George Washington 80

V

Van Buren, Martin 150
Vawter, Charles 54
Vawter, Clara S. Peck 54
Vawter, Eliza Lively Gwinn 57
Vawter, George W. 54, 57
Vawter, John Henderson 54
Vawter, Lewis 54
Victorian style 1, 8-9, 22, 26, 28, 46, 57, 70, 80, 94, 103, 106, 133-35, 171
Virginia and Tennessee Railroad 13
Virginia Assembly 87
Virginia Polytechnic Institute and State University 87
Virginia Railroad 111

W

Wayside, West Virginia 22, 38
Webb, Louise D. Bivens 141
Welch, West Virginia 167
Wesley, Benjamin Franklin 45, 74
Wesley, Florence Mary Miller 13, 46, 70, 74, 82, 147, 175
Wesley, Fred 46, 70, 74, 82
Wesley, Glenna Lee 46
Wesley Hollow (Holler) 1, 5, 45, 77
Wesley, Martha Jane Skaggs 74
Wesley, Saphronia E. Houchins 45, 74
West Virginia Legislature 108
Wheeler, Billy and Melva 145
Whitten, Burl 74
Whitten, Calvin Scotland 74
Wickline, Sara Jane Ballard (Susie) 93
Willow Bend 35
Wilson Mill Road 91, 94,
Witt, Doc 142
Woods Fort 91
Woodson Road 133
Woodson, Sue 143
Woodson, W. O. 142
Wright, Frank A. 8
Wright, Frank Lloyd 9
Wyoming County, West Virginia 47, 74

Y

Young, Nancy Peck (Nannie) 41
Young, George P. 41-42

Image Index

Arnott, R. H. 31
Arnott, Robert H., home 29-30
Ballard & Arnott Store 31
Ballard Maggie 28, 30
Ballard, Helen 28
Ballard, Issac N. 27-31
Ballard, Issac N., home 26-27
Ballard, Kate May Walkup 27
Ballard, Mabel M., home 93-94
Ballard, Paul 30
Ballard, Roy 30
Ballard, Ruth 30
Ballard, Stella 30
Ballard Food Center 43-44
Bivens, Charlie, home 131-32
Bivens, Frank C., home 140-42
Broyles, John A., home 92
Broyles, Minnie Pearl Calloway 56-57
Broyles, Samuel Overton, home 145-46
Broyles, Samuel Overton 146
Broyles, Wilbur, I. 57
Broyles, Wilbur, I., home 56
Campbell, Dr. Lewis, home 155-56
Campbell/Long, home 157-59
Cashmere 130
Coulter home 107
Dillon, Katheryn, home 100-1
Dunlap, Addison, home 41-53
Dunlap, Addison, outbuildings 53
Dunlap, Elizabeth Patterson (Libbie) 25
Dunlap, Marion 25
Dunlap, Robert S, home 22-25
Dunn, Arthur D., home 133
Dunn, Charles, home 160
Dunn, Eli Harold, home 134
Dunn, Marshall B,. home 135
E. I. Terry Store 118-19
Ellison, A. D., Sr. 69
Ellison, Addison 69
Ellison, Addison, home 67
Ellison, Charles I., home 63
Ellison, early home 65
Ellison, Harriet 67
Ellison, John Zachariah 68
Ellison, John Zachariah, home 66-67

Ellison, Judy 49
Ellison, Richard Warren 49
Farley, Burnice, home 147
Fleshman, Janie Sheppe, home 161-62
Fleshman, Janie Sheppe, music 162
Garrison, Sam, shoe shop 23
Gwinn, Bessie 60
Hansbarger, Will, home 102
Hansbarger, John Echols 103-4
Heslep, Clarence O., home 122-23, 125
Heslep, Jenny 125
Heslep Mill 124
Hines, Charles Albert, home 138-39
Humphreys Store 153-4
Hunter, Dr. John O. and Hunter, Dr. Will 117
Hunter, Dr. John, home 115-16
Hunter, Dr. John, office 117
Johnson, Eddy 38
Johnson, Ethel (Sis) 38
Johnson, Georgia Young 37
Johnson, Gertrude 38
Johnson, John R. (Jack), home 35-37
Johnson, John R. (Jack) 37-38
Johnson, Lucille 38
Johnson, Sally 38
Larew, Robert 60
Level, Barbara Ellison 49
Lively, Leonidas, home 88-89
Long Store 32
Maddy, Frank, home 33-34
Map: Western Monroe County, WV 5
McDaniel, John A. 99
McDaniel, John A., home 95-98
McDaniel, Mary Ann Humphreys 99
Measimore, Clara 66
Miller, Adison Plunkett (Plunk), home 82-85
Miller, Dewey Gordon 6, 12
Miller, George Dewey 6
Miller, John Campbell 6, 10, 12, 15
Miller, John Campbell, furniture 84-85
Miller, Florence, tables 86
Miller, John Campbell, home 70-75
Miller, John Clyde 6, 12

Miller, Lee 55
Miller, Letcher E. 55
Miller, Letcher E., home 54-55
Miller, Lillie Belle 6
Miller, Ray Seleska 6, 12
Miller/Wesley farm 73
N & W homes, Pageton, West Virginia 168
N & W homes, Elkhorn, West Virginia 169-70
Orchard Store 81
Patton, John Parker, home 106
Pence, Dewey E., home 47-9
Pence, Mary Jane Neal, home 40-41
Peterstown Bank 120-21
Peterstown School 112-13
Red Sulphur Springs Church 151-52
Riner, John Thompson 79
Riner, John Thompson, home 79
Riner, Robert E., home 39
Ryan, Dr. Dorsey McNeil, home 163
Ryan, Dr. Dorsey McNeil, office 164-5
Ryan, John R., home 78
Spangler, Cliff, home 127
Spangler, Fred Clark 127
Spangler, Emily Crotshin 127
Symns, Clarence, home 108-9
Symns, Clarence 109
Terry, E. I., home 114
Underwood, George W., home 80
Vawter, Eliza 60
Vawter, George 60
Vawter, George, home 57-60
Vawter, Josephine 60
Vawter, Robert G. 59-61
Wesley, Florence Mary Miller 6, 73
Wesley, Fred 73, 76
Wesley, Sephronia 76
Young, George, P., home 42-43

About the Authors

Author and educator Becky Hatcher Crabtree lives in Monroe County, West Virginia, near Lindside, in the midst of these artistic reminders of rural America's history. She writes on the front porch of one of John Campbell Miller's houses where she and husband Roger live. Their three daughters grew up there and now five grandchildren roam the fields and climb the trees and limestone outcroppings much like rural West Virginia's children have for centuries. Currently, she teaches science at nearby James Monroe High School and helps tend a mountain farm complete with sheep, chickens, dogs, and one cat. In addition to watching high school sports, gardening, and reading, she participates in  environmental activism, and advocates for unheard voices. Previous works include *Alaska Hoops, Tales from the Girls' Locker Room*, a collection of essays; a fictional trilogy set in Monroe County, *Drunk on Peace and Quiet, Hungover with Grandma*, and *Pick Your Poison*; and a biography, *Try and Be Somebody: The Story of Dr. Henry Lake Dickason*.

 Fred Ziegler retired in 2003 from teaching and researching Historical Geology and Paleogeography at the University of Chicago, and moved to West Virginia, where he and his wife Barbara bought "Cook's Old Mill," in Greenville. He became interested in local history and has written books on *The Carriages of Monroe, West Virginia*, and the *Settlement of the Greater Greenbrier Valley*. He has served as the president of the Monroe County Historical Society and spearheaded the building of the Carriage House Museum in Union. The museum now has eight full-size horse-drawn vehicles, including an Omnibus, which at one time conveyed visitors to the resort spas at Sweet Springs and Chalybeate Springs. Future book projects include *The History of Red Sulphur Springs, Monroe County*.

35th Star Publishing
Charleston, West Virginia
www.35thstar.com

www.ingramcontent.com/pod-product-compliance
Lightning Source LLC
Chambersburg PA
CBHW081835170426
43199CB00017B/2735